Tales from the Big Thicket

# TALES FROM THE Big Thicket

EDITED BY
Francis E. Abernethy

UNIVERSITY OF TEXAS PRESS
AUSTIN AND LONDON

Library of Congress Catalog Card No. 66–30013
Copyright © 1966 by Francis E. Abernethy

Type set by Southwestern Typographics, Inc., Dallas
Printed by the University of Texas Printing Division, Austin
Bound by Universal Bookbindery, Inc., San Antonio

1. Cecil Overstreet.

## FOREWORD

*Tales from the Big Thicket* is dedicated to the people of Kountze
and of Hardin County and to Cecil Overstreet, who introduced me
to these woods and who, to me, best represents the Thicket, past
and present. The Overstreets came to the Big Thicket in 1852 and
settled near Honey Island. Since then they have scattered their
bones and blood all through this part of the country. Cecil's family
has figured one way or another, good or bad, in everything that has
happened in the Thicket. And Cecil is a hard runner and an all-day
hunter, a fit representative of a long line of fighters and hunters
who have roamed the Big Thicket for over a hundred years. He
has my greatest respect.

Most of the tales that follow come straight out of the Thicket
and are written by people who are a part of it. They are kin to the
Thicket and every old family that passed through it. The tuft grass
and the white oak, the deer and the yellow hammers are their ancestors who have gone their subtle ways and have turned and

are passing again. And the tall pines are the old settlers, still there looking over them, seeing how they are getting along.

The research for this book was financed by the Lamar Tech Research Center under the consecutive directorships of Dr. R. V. Andrews and Mr. Lloyd Cherry. I appreciate very much the Center's assistance and encouragement; there are not many places where a man can get mileage to attend a fox hunt or a fiddling contest.

I particularly thank Professor Wilson M. Hudson of The University of Texas and the Texas Folklore Society for getting this book started and for operating the tedious machinery that finally got it to the press.

The Big Thicket Association, under the present leadership of Mayor Dempsie Henley of Liberty, is now the center of Thicket research and conservation; I thank the Association for its interest. Arden Hooks and Lance Rosier showed me much in the Thicket that my own city-dimmed eyes were not able to see. Lois Parker, Ruth Scurlock, Aline House, Dempsie Henley, Thomas Sidney Hooks, and Ethel Osborn Hill are other collectors of Thicket lore who generously shared their holdings with me. Marion Springer typed and proofread ably and patiently. Luther Lowery furnished bed and board. I thank all of these and I especially thank the contributors, whose experiences and lives in the Big Thicket have been just as interesting as those they write about.

FRANCIS EDWARD ABERNETHY
*Stephen F. Austin State College*
*Nacogdoches, Texas*

# CONTENTS

ILLUSTRATIONS

MAPS

# Tales from the Big Thicket

# THE BIG THICKET: An Introduction

BY FRANCIS E. ABERNETHY

I guess the Big Thicket is as much a product of the imagination and wishful thinking as it is a geographical area. It represents the Great Unknown to the mind cluttered with trade names in a society labeled and categorized. It is a happy hunting ground for the mind, and in man's fancy the cool green womb to which he can retreat from the hot panic of concrete and glass in the industrialized brick jungles we call cities. It is the individual's final fortress against civilization.

To those who talk about it, the Big Thicket stands for something else too; it is the lair of the mysterious. According to the stories about the place, there is no telling what a man might come across, in the shape of man or beast, if he wanders deep enough into those woods. Before I had ever seen the Thicket I had been told that if I walked into it out of sight of the road I would get lost, and I have found out since then that this statement was pretty close to right. On a cloudy day or when the sun is at the top of the sky, the mind's compass points are easily shifted around; and panic tries to get hold of a man when he starts wondering whether he is walking deeper into the Thicket or out of it—or when he hits a trail that he doesn't recognize. A man by the name of Hendrix one foggy night strayed off a Thicket trail that he had been walking for forty years, and

2. Sunrise on Village Creek.

searchers didn't find him till eight days later. It hasn't been many
years ago when a young fellow got lost and the fright of the Thicket scared him out of his head. His rescuers had to rope him to bring
him in. Governor Sul Ross got lost in the Thicket in the eighties
and spent the night and a couple of days in the woods until Fount
Simmons found him and led him out. At the present time Henry
Overstreet, the sheriff of Hardin County, keeps a pack of bloodhounds ready to go to the aid of those who get confused in the
Thicket.

4

3. Claude Davenport and the Hardin County Sheriff's Department bloodhounds.

4. Water moccasin.

They also said down at the barber shop that a man couldn't walk a hundred yards into the brush without being snake bitten. That was an exaggeration; no more people are bitten in the Thicket area than in other places that have large snake populations. But there are some good chances to get snake bitten in the Thicket if a fellow is looking for the experience. Scattered throughout the Thicket are small weed-choked ponds, the frogging grounds for stump-tailed cottonmouth moccasins. They lie in the coontail and spatterdock with just their fist-sized heads protruding, the mean eye gazing over the smiling white lip. Or roll a log in the early spring; the canebrake rattler hibernates late and lies in a tight coil of black chevrons on shiny grey, waiting till he thaws out enough to shake his rattles before he will come forth to hunt. A small but distant

5. Coral snake.

6. Canebrake rattler. (Courtesy Ernest Tanzer)

7. Copperhead.

8. Pigmy rattler.

cousin of his, the pigmy rattler, can winter under a pine knot. Lift the loose, thick bark of a fallen and rotting oak tree; the long secret that feeds on the insects and larvae of this tree-trunk world is banded red, yellow, and black, and is the coral snake. Lying flat on a golden-brown blanket of pine needles is the golden-brown copperhead, the cottonmouth's cousin who can blend in with his surroundings as well as his kinsman. These are the snakes you are warned about; there are other reptiles of the same build that can materialize under your feet in the dark water-soaked leaves of the Thicket floor. They are good for the jump effect.

A lot of reports of bear and panther come out of the Thicket, and everybody who has hunted there has considered the possibility of one or the other coming over his stand. As for me, I have yet to see a sign of either. In fact, I'd give a panther one free jump at me just so I could go back to town and say I'd seen one. But I do believe they are there; or at least I hope they are there. There are good reports to that effect. Abe Overstreet saw a panther during deer season two years ago. He was leaning up against a sweet-gum tree late one evening waiting for a buck to cross an old logging road, when he heard movement in the brush about 150 feet ahead. He clicked off his safety and watched as a doe nervously slipped out of the myrtle and ran down the road and into the thicket on the other side. He noticed a movement in the myrtle where the doe had come from and saw an antlerless silhouette which he took to be another doe. By the time the silhouette became an animal running down the old road and the animal became recognizable as a panther, it was out of range of Abe's shotgun.

Several bears have been seen. Two cubs were reported in the Thicket on the Kountze-Sour Lake Road near Little Pine Island Bayou. Emmett Lack, the state representative, claims he hit one with his car when he was returning to Kountze about four o'clock one morning. Old man Ramer, a commercial fisherman who lives on a houseboat where Village Creek runs into the Neches River, jumped one last spring. He said he and his dog were 'coon hunting on Village that night and he could tell that his dog was getting nervous and didn't want to hunt out from him. Finally the dog

9. Old Man Ramer.

winded something and headed toward it halfheartedly. Mr. Ramer
followed and soon met the dog squawling back to him, hackles
raised, and tail between his legs. The old man, who is best characterized by the fact that he pulls his own teeth with pliers and fish-
ing cord, moved ahead to see what could be fierce enough to scare
his dog. By the time he got there all that was left was a bunch of
tracks in the sand by the creek's edge, but they were bear tracks

and their maker was gone to hide out in the Thicket and maybe not be heard of for another year or two.

Big Thicket stories will also warn you about the people who live in the Thicket or on the edge of it, and there is some basis in history for this warning. The Thicket has always been a hide-out. The last of the Atakapans and some of the Karankawas who were being run off their traditional hunting grounds moved toward the Big Thicket. During the Texas Revolution Sam Houston was prepared to hide the Texan Army in the Thicket if he lost at San Jacinto. And not all of these settlers that moved into the Thicket in the 1840's and 1850's were going there because they liked mosquitoes; some of them were hiding out. The Thicket became a good place to go if you needed to be scarce for a while. There was some difference even about these other settlers, those who weren't running from the law. They were typical of first-wave settlers, and their kind was described two hundred years ago by William Byrd and St. Jean de Crèvecoeur. They were getting away from people and from the rules and restrictions that people put on life. They were the warriors and hunters, the antisocials, and the introverts who were always moving west ahead of the confines of society; and if a Thicketlike area were to turn up today in some uncharted part of Mexico, half of Hardin County would move down there to start all over again.

The Big Thicket became particularly famous as a hide-out during the Civil War when the Jayhawkers, as Big Thicket residents still call them, took to the big woods to keep from going to the war. The big fire that Captain Kaiser set to burn them out of the Thicket is still sort of smouldering in Hardin County.

One character who helped in recent years to give the Thicket a reputation was referred to in area newspapers as "The Nude Man of the Big Thicket." Most of the stories about this individual go back to the early 1950's. Several people had caught glimpses of this hermit, and one day Mr. Sutton, who lives on the edge of the Thicket proper, met the man coming down the road. He described the nudist as a large man, deeply tanned and hairy, with a long beard. The two walked together down the road for about a hun-

11

10. Lance Rosier.

dred yards, and Mr. Sutton told the man that he was going to report him to the law. The man, who had a gun in each hand, told him that he had been living in the Thicket for three years and if the law came after him, they'd have to come shooting. This story, as I heard it, runs out here and blends in with a tale told by Mrs. C. C. Riser about an escaped mental patient found in the Thicket in October, 1954, who had lived there for nine years on armadillo and wild berries.

The point is that the Thicket is one of the last places in the United States where this kind of story can get started. It is roped off from the general public by briars and ty-vine and by myrtle and yaupon thickets that you have to crawl through on your hands and knees. And I hope it stays that way.

There are just about as many stories about where the Thicket is as there are about what is in it. In the early days the Big Thicket name was applied to an area of climax forest that was bounded on the north by the Camino Real, on the east by the Sabine River, on the south by the Gulf Coastal prairie, and on the west by the Brazos. The Spanish missionaries described the area as an impenetrable wilderness. The early settlers began moving in on it, however, and found that it wasn't as bad as the stories made it out to be. The Big Thicket was not destroyed on its edges; it was merely further and more closely defined. By the 1840's the Thicket was recognized for what and where it was, and the offspring of its first settlers follow the teachings of their ancestors and their own experience in establishing the Big Thicket boundaries.

According to one old bear hunter, Mr. Carter Hart, the Thicket is fifty miles long. It begins near the corner post where the Polk, Liberty, and Hardin county lines meet, and runs in a south-easterly direction following the Pine Island Bayou drainage to below and east of Sour Lake. The land is hilly up north of the Thicket in Polk and Tyler counties, and the dirt is red. There are more hickory-nut and red oaks in these hills than the sweet gum, pin oaks and gum that grow so easily in the Thicket. And there are more seeps and springs on those hillsides than can be found in the flat land to the south. The water that trickles out of the red hills starts a half a dozen or more creeks that open out into the wide-fan top of the Thicket. Menard Creek is the main one and the Thicket traditionally begins in the Menard Creek area, but other creeks that start or flow up there at the beginning are Mill Creek, Meetinghouse Branch, Beaver Creek, Little Pine Island, Union Wells, Bad Luck, and Big Sandy. And there is legend in every one of them.

The most important body of water in the Thicket, though, is Pine Island Bayou. It begins rather weakly in the spring creek area in the northwest part of Hardin County and strains itself through cypress knees all the way down through the Thicket till the woods play out at the Black Creek junction in the rice fields northwest of Beaumont, and the bayou spills its water into the Neches.

On a map that shows elevation, the boundaries of the Thicket can be seen to stay pretty well in the Pine Island Bayou drainage and in the drainage of the creeks that parallel it or empty into it— Black Creek, Steep Bank, Tenmile, and Little Pine Island Bayou.

13

The Thicket is that flat, grey-clay, poorly drained land that spreads on either side of Pine Island Bayout to below Sour Lake, where it thins out in stands of tall pine and is finally chopped off by the large rice farms of the Coastal prairie.

The Thicket was easier to define in the old days before loggers came. On the north in the Polk and Tyler county hills was a climax forest of hardwoods, of ash, hickory, white oaks, and walnuts a hundred feet high, that grew together at the tops and shaded out all secondary growth. The forest floor was clean. The virgin pine stands to the east of the Thicket were clean too, and the great pines, six feet in diameter at breast high, ruled the sand hills that rose between Village Creek and the Neches. The old-timers say that you could build a good-sized house out of one pine tree in those days. Neither climax forest—hardwood to the north or pine to the east—was considered to be a part of the Thicket because the brush wasn't thick. The land under the trees was open.

There was the big Coastal prairie to the south of the Thicket where wild horses and cattle grazed, and the Batson Prairie held back the Big Thicket on the southwest. A western limit is harder to draw. At one time there was a stand of big pines that followed the Trinity drainage, but now that is gone and the Thicket-type timber has moved all the way to the banks of the Trinity. But the heart of the Big Thicket stops before you get to the Trinity going west.

The Big Thicket has been pretty well cut over, but the land is as tough as its people and you can't knock it down so that it won't get back up again. The Thicket is still thick. The pin oaks and water oaks and sweet-gum trees grow tall and rank, straining to get up out of the underbrush and into the light and air above. Laurel bushes and yaupon bunch together in the forest's middle world. The magnolia's dark green squats among its taller neighbors. A may-haw patch, two or three acres around, blooms dainty white in early March and drops its fruit in the water of the late April creek rises. Chinquapin trees so big you can't reach around them sit on hummocks that swell above the surrounding flats, and sweet bays spotted with their rich white blossoms stand hip-deep in a flooded baygall. Cypress trees edge the creek banks and poke their knees up through the old slough beds. Palmetto higher than your head rattles in the wind. And tying everything together are the vines: smilax, ty-vine, poison ivy, saw briars, muscadine and grape vines at every level.

The Big Thicket is still thick, and its depths are still as mysterious and forbidding as they were when the first settler came to live on corn and sweet potatoes, bear meat and venison. The little, black, angry bees still hive in the hollows, and the buck deer leave their big scrapes on the dim woods trails. Wild hogs that can rip a man from ankle to appetite still root for mast in the pin oak flats. And if you are desperate enough, here is one last place where you can find a hiding place till the trouble blows over.

# A SKETCH OF THE GEOLOGY AND
# SOILS OF THE BIG THICKET

BY SAUL ARONOW

The Big Thicket, which occupies a major part of
Hardin County and portions of the adjoining Polk,
Liberty, and Jefferson Counties (see map facing p. 12), is very
young as the geologist measures time. The clays and sands that
support the extensive forest of the Thicket are perhaps less than a
million years old. At this writing the best estimate of the age of the
earth—an estimate based on the slow decay of radioactive elements
—is about 4,500 million years. The past million years of this history
certainly have been most eventful in producing the familiar features of southeast Texas. All of the coastal features such as deltas,
barrier islands, bays, marshes, and lagoons were formed during
this time. Also made during this period were the extensive high-
stream terraces bordering the flood plains of the Sabine, Neches,
Trinity, San Jacinto, and Brazos rivers, which supply most of the
sand and gravel to southeast Texas.

Outside the Gulf Coast region, during the past million years,
vast continental glaciers have spread at least four times from cen-
tral Canada into the midwestern and northeastern parts of the
United States, while in the west large glaciers descended from the
Rocky Mountains and the coast ranges into adjacent lowlands.
Most other continents were similarly glaciated. Geologists have

11. Saul Aronow.

given the name "Pleistocene" to this time of the glaciers. Sometimes, an older name, "Quaternary," is used instead.

The clays and sands of the Big Thicket, then, were deposited during the time of the Pleistocene glaciers. To begin with, over a million years ago the waters of the Gulf of Mexico were rolling over the Thicket area. Gradually, however, deltaic plains, with fringing marine deposits, were laid down by the Pleistocene ancestor of the present Trinity River. (Similar deltaic plains are being deposited today by the nearby Brazos, Rio Grande, and Mississippi Rivers.) And gradually, as the deposition continued, the water retreated and the land of the Thicket appeared.

The deltaic and associated marine sediments found in the Thicket were originally classified as two geologic formations, the Beaumont Clay and the Lissie Formation. Recently, some geologists, with purer motives than to confound the uninitiated, have subdivided the Lissie into an Upper and Lower Lissie, giving us three

17

12. Climax hardwoods in Boggy Creek bottom.

geologic formations. They are in relative age from youngest to oldest, the Beaumont Clay, the Upper Lissie and the Lower Lissie.

Now, it might well be asked what relevance the advance and retreat of the glaciers have to the abandoned deltaic plains under the Thicket and their division into three separate formations. Geologists believe that during the times of the advances of the great glaciers the sea level went down, perhaps as much as 450 feet below its present level. The best explanation for this lowering of sea level is that much water from the oceans was incorporated into the glaciers and thus transferred to the surface of the continents. The shoreline of the Gulf of Mexico was then many miles out in the present Gulf, with much of the continental shelf exposed. All of the major streams in the Gulf Coast, as well as in the rest of the world, cut deep channels. The floors of some of these are now partly or completely filled but they remain below present sea level. Sabine Lake, Trinity Bay, and Corpus Christi Bay are the partly obliterated remnants of such channels. Other streams, such as the Brazos and Rio Grande, carrying more sediments, have long since filled theirs. When the glaciers melted and sea level rose again, the streams began depositing the deltaic plains. The three formations in the Thicket record three of these rises of sea level between glaciations.

The boundary between the Beaumont Clay and the two other formations is perhaps the easiest of the formation boundaries to discern, for farm-to-market road 787 between Saratoga and Fuqua more or less follows it. The boundary is marked by a scarp about twenty-five or thirty feet high. In a few places, this scarp has been eroded by streams and the road descends to lower levels—for example, where the road crosses Little Pine Island Bayou about three miles southeast of Thicket. South and west of the road, and below the scarp, lies the Beaumont Clay; north and east, the Upper and Lower Lissie. About halfway between Votaw and Fuqua, roughly at the Hardin-Liberty county line, the road makes its final descent onto the surface of the Beaumont Clay.

The boundary between the Upper and Lower Lissie Formations is not marked by any clear-cut scarp, but rather by some subtle changes of slope which can best be seen on a detailed topographic map. Within the Thicket area, the boundary may run from where Doe Pond Creek enters Little Pine Island Bayou east to Honey Island, and then to Kountze.

The soils in the Big Thicket, and the underlying parent clays and sands from which the soils developed, are rather similar. Most are

19

13. Hickory Creek.

acid forest soils belonging to the Red-Yellow Podzolic group and
to associated hydromorphic soils (that is, soils whose main characteristics are due to poor drainage). The upper or surface parts of
these soils include sandy loams and loamy sands; the lower parts
and parent materials are mostly sandy clay loams, many with red

or black shot-sized and larger ironstone concretions or nodules. Virtually no differences can be seen between samples from the Upper and the Lower Lissie. However, below the scarp in the Beaumont Clay, soils and parent materials consisting mainly of clay and containing concretions or nodules of calcium carbonate are common. Such soils, referred to as "Grumosols," seem to be absent from the Lissie, at least in the Thicket area.

It should be noted that soil scientists have recently dropped the terms "Red-Yellow Podzolic" soils and "Grumosols." Readers of some recent soil surveys and reports may find these referred to as "Ultisols" and "Vertisols," respectively.

Most of the area of the Big Thicket is poorly drained because of low slopes and impervious materials within or below the soils.

The general background of the geology of the Thicket can be read about in Bernard and LeBlanc (1965). Details of this geology are not available in print and as given here reflect the writer's unpublished field work for the Texas Bureau of Economic Geology. Information on the soils can be obtained from the published soils surveys of Polk County (Smith *et al.*, 1930) and of Jefferson County (Crout *et al.*, 1965), and from the reconnaissance or soil association maps of Hardin and Liberty counties available from the U.S. Soil Conservation Service.

*References*

Bernard, H. A., and R. J. LeBlanc, "Resume of the Quaternary Geology of the Northwestern Gulf of Mexico," pp. 137–185 in *The Quaternary of the United States* (H. E. Wright and D. G. Frey, eds.). New Jersey: Princeton University Press, 1965.

Crout, Jack, D. G. Symmank, and G. A. Peterson. *Soil Survey of Jefferson County, Texas*. U.S. Department of Agriculture Series, No. 21. Washington, D.C.: Government Printing Office, 1960.

Smith, H. M., T. C. Reitch, Harvey Oakes, L. G. Ragsdale, and A. H. Bean. *Soil Survey of Polk County, Texas*. U.S. Department of Agriculture Series, No. 36. Washington, D.C.: Government Printing Office, 1930.

21

# FOLKLORE IN THE BIG THICKET

BY ARCHER FULLINGIM

*Archer Fullingim is editor, printer, and publisher of* THE KOUNTZE NEWS. *He is also a fire-brand Democrat who can raise more Cain with Republicans and with Birchites in his one editorial column than all the rest of Texas' liberal newspapers combined. In the Thicket he is a controversial figure, sworn at as often and as vigorously as he is sworn by.*

*Archer's writing style is his own, very personal and idiomatic rather than grammatically pure and journalistically bland. His news stories, as well as his editorials, tumble along like the energetic and rapid-fire monologues which he sometimes delivers to his visitors.*

*The Printer writes and talks about everything in the Thicket. Banner headlines will announce that a bear or panther has been spotted in the nearby woods; or a lead will pose the question, "Do Panthers Scream?" Several issues will be devoted to both sides of this problem. He can write an exciting front-page story about the size of watermelons or the shape of gourds raised in the Thicket. And he will top it all off with a front-page character sketch—and a three-column picture—of the Barefoot Man from Caney Head. Archer is one of the few journalists who has had the courage to allow his own personality to be a part of his paper, and I wouldn't miss a single issue.—F.E.A.*

14. Archer Fullingim.

I live in Kountze, Hardin County, Texas, which advertises itself on billboards, on chamber-of-commerce literature, and in *The Kountze News* as "The Town with a Sense of Humor" and "The Big Light in the Big Thicket." Kountze consciously tries to live up to the first slogan, though, as a matter of fact, I often think there is less humor in Kountze than in any other place I know. The slogan did have a rich beginning and probably some basis in fact, even though nobody can prove it; but then to my way of thinking that is the ideal way for folklore to get started.

When I moved to Hardin County twenty years ago, about the first thing I heard was that Kountze's slogan was "the town with a sense of humor," that this slogan had been decided on in the last century, and that it would be no use for the new newspaper to try to think up another slogan. "We are not the gateway to anything," people said. "Nor are we a queen city or any kind of a jewel of the forest."

The son of the man who was supposed to have originated the slogan told me how many of the streets were named in "the town with the sense of humor." He said that his father, Ben Hooks, who owned a general store and was one of Kountze's two leading citizens, was a great fiddler, as was the other leading citizen. Often they would sit up all night and play the fiddle. They owned most of the town, especially along the railroad tracks. When it became necessary to name the streets, they named them after animals and trees and plants of the Big Thicket, in which Kountze was and still is a clearing. They gave the streets such names as Bear, Fox, Cherry, and Deer. The main street is Pine Street. Some of the names have been abandoned because they didn't look well in print, so you won't find street names like Skunk, Polecat, Shittim, Boar Coon, or Pisselm on the map today. Three other street names never did make the new map either. They were Panther Scream, Ima Hogg, and Ura Hogg.

Periodically in Hardin County there rage in the columns of *The Kountze News* (which I publish) vitriolic word battles over whether or not a panther screams like a woman. Somebody will come in and say that he saw a panther in the Thicket (and it's always a black panther), and he will say that it screamed like a hysterical, frightened woman.

As I say, this happens two or three times a year. Always it gets a rise out of panther experts in Dallas, Houston, Beaumont, Wyoming, and Arizona, who send in long letters—backed, of course, by the *National Geographic Magazine* and encyclopedias—arguing that there is no such thing as a black panther, and that a panther never, never screams, especially like a fear-crazed woman.

In the Big Thicket country old-timers are convinced that when someone died in the old days and was laid out in the residence to await burial, a black panther would always mount the gatepost and scream bloody murder like a woman and that all the house cats would rush under the bed and the dogs under the house, whimpering. Nearly everybody in the Big Thicket fervently believes that panthers may be tawny in color every other place, but that in the Big Thicket they are coal black with scarlet mouths and scarlet tongues, and with eyes that shine in the dark. They also believe that panthers scream like a woman, and you can find hundreds of people who have heard panthers scream.

The town of Kountze got its slogan during the administration of Governor James Stephen Hogg. It was believed then that the governor had two daughters, named Ima and Ura Hogg; so our two early residents, believing this and wishing to honor the governor, used the names of his daughters as street names, along with names taken from the fauna and flora of the Big Thicket.

A little while back I reviewed Robert C. Cotner's biography of Governor Hogg in my column in *The Kountze News*. In my long review I mentioned casually that when I was growing up I was told that the governor had two daughters named Ima and Ura, and that I believed it for years, until I learned conclusively in correspondence with Mr. Cotner that Hogg had only one daughter, named Ima. Actually, Mr. Cotner was rather put out that I had asked him about the mythical Ura; he did not mention the Ura matter in the Hogg biography.

Immediately after I published the review, I began to get indignant calls protesting that Mr. Cotner was mistaken, that the caller lived on what used to be Ura Hogg Street. I even received a few letters berating me for publishing such a big lie for school children to read and believe. To get letters from the denizens of the Big Thicket is very unusual—they almost always come in to tell me face to face what a big liar I am. They seldom write.

It was useless for me to tell them there never was a Ura Hogg. I even wrote Mr. Cotner, as I said, expressing surprise that he did not mention the folklore about Ura in his 600-page book. My letter did not sit well with him, and he criticized me for even suggesting that he had been derelict in not exploding the Ura Hogg myth in his book.

I will have to admit that a lot of residents of the Big Thicket lost all confidence in my integrity. When I published Mr. Cotner's letter to me, it seemed to support the thesis that I was trying to hand my readers a lot of hanky-panky.

The piney-wood rooter, a species of wild hog, is one of the heroes of the Big Thicket. This hog is given credit for the discovery of oil at Saratoga. One of the first families in the county, the Cottons, came to Saratoga long before the Civil War. Their hogs kept coming in with oil mud caked on their sides. The Cottons found the place, and there is where the first Saratoga gushers were brought in.

The real hero of the Big Thicket is still the Louisiana bear, which has been extinct in the Thicket for at least thirty-five years. In 1905 the man who gave Kountze its slogan, Ben Hooks, and his brother Bud killed fifteen bears. The next year the great hunter Ben Lilly hunted bear in the Thicket with these brothers. Last year a man brought me a picture of what he said was the tree in which the last bear was shot in 1927.

They hunt fox in the Thicket now, but the big stories for sixty years in Hardin County were of the super battles between a bear hound named Dandy and the big bears. People still tell how Dandy would lead and drive a bear to where the hunter with the gun stood.

Much of the folklore about bears in the Thicket has to do with people who have got lost in the dense woods. One such story has it that a small two-year-old baby was lost for weeks and when it was finally found it was under the jealous care of a great she-bear, and was in good health and fat and sassy. The night the baby was rescued, the story goes, the she-bear had no difficulty in tracing it to the house in the clearing in the forest. She tried to break into the house and the father had to kill her to keep her from coming in after the baby. Then there are stories of super bears, one-eyed or footless after battles with traps and dogs, and there is one story of a bear who hated the man who had shot and wounded him but had failed to kill him. This bear tormented the farmer for years, killing

15.  A piney-woods rooter.

his calves and colts and destroying his crops. Bears and hogs throughout the Thicket are invested with human characteristics.

The Big Thicket also has its ghost road. Only five years ago two thousand people came in a three-day period to see the luminous ball float down this road—after I had published a story in *The Kountze News* about the Bragg Light. Old-timers said it was the ghost of a slain Mexican section hand on the old railroad, which after the Saratoga oil boom collapsed was changed into a straight seven-mile auto road into Saratoga. The crowds quit coming after I published the explanations of geologists that the luminous balls were gaseous substances arising from the swamps of the surrounding Thicket, and I was thoroughly hated for printing a logical explanation.

One of the most widely publicized stories of the Thicket concerns what is known as the Kaiser Burnout near Honey Island. According to fact and legend—and the two are now inseparable— about seventy-five Confederate army deserters hid out during the Civil War in the Thicket near Honey Island. A Captain Kaiser was sent from Galveston to capture the deserters and return them to the Confederate army or shoot them. He cornered them in a section of the Thicket near Honey Island and burned them out, but he captured only a few after killing two. This story was the subject of a WPA play by Larry Fisher in the 1930's, but despite extensive research no documented history of the episode is now available.

Honey Island got its name at the time. The families of the deserters would hang food for them in the trees on a rise of ground. These were bee trees and the men partly subsisted on honey from the trees. Honey Island now has two huge twin swimming pools fed from an ancient artesian well. The Bragg ghost road is only a few miles away.

Several years ago, I ran a small story in the paper that raised the question of how Pigeon Roost Prairie, about four miles from Kountze, got its name. For six weeks afterward, in every issue of

16. Pigeon Roost Prairie.

*The Kountze News*, I published fascinating versions of what
great-grandfathers had told grandfathers and what grandfathers
had told sons. Some said that carrier pigeons came over by the millions—and that John James Audubon swore they did—and roosted
in the great pine trees of the virgin forest, and that the droppings
were so thick, sometimes twelve feet, that the trees were killed.

Others contended that the prairie was there all the time—the
argument raged for months. I must have published in all enough
material to fill a book on the subject. A number of writers, biolo-

29

gists, and even folklorists wrote learned articles for me. In the end, it was generally agreed that fantastic numbers of pigeons did actually roost in the trees and that their droppings did kill the trees. I looked up what Audubon himself had said about passenger pigeons in this area and published it as a final article. He wrote that he had devised an accurate method of counting carrier pigeons and that in one day he counted 238 million pigeons flying overhead in Louisiana.

In the Kountze Public Library there is a very good bas-relief sculpture of a man winning a foot race against a horse. His name is Gus Hooks. The story goes that he was the fastest foot-runner in the country. People came from all over East Texas to run against him. One day after he had outrun a man from Louisiana who had a considerable reputation, he said, "I can outrun your horse too, you and your horse and you on him." They say that he did just that. They say that he would get ahead of the man and his horse and turn around and run backward, taunting the rider on the horse. They say that the race was from the saloon to Cypress Creek, at least a mile.

Gus is also credited with burning down the old Hardin County courthouse at Old Hardin, four miles from Kountze, and then running back to his home six miles east on Village Creek and getting in bed before his expected accusers could catch up with him. The only clue was that someone had seen a man running with incredible speed from the burning, kerosene-splashed courthouse. Who else could run like Gus? They said that he was paid to do it by people who wanted to move the courthouse to Kountze. His accusers mounted horses and rode on the run to his house but found him snoring when they got there. A few months later a new courthouse was built, in Kountze.

Gus was a man of unconventional habits. He was well to do but he always wore overalls. When he drank whiskey he would drink it out of a brown soft-drink bottle then popular; when he drank soft drinks he would drink them out of a whiskey bottle. He was an expert at tending bees; he could lead a swarm of bees ten miles.

People still describe how he would be seen herding the bees like a sheep dog, running back and forth and talking to the bees and waving at them. It was believed that he kept all his money—which was all in gold—in his beehives, and that the bees would sting everybody but him.

My friend Robert Stanley Coe, who is related to all the people I have been talking about, tells of a trip he made through the Thicket some twenty-five years ago. Armed with only a compass, he was walking with a companion directly across the Thicket. What they had decided to do was to go in at one side and come out on the other. That would take two days. They knew they would come to a house about the time they got thirsty. They knew where the house was, and that's the way it turned out.

They asked the woman in the yard for a drink of water. She was wearing a split bonnet that hid her face. She went to the well and drew up a fresh bucket of water and handed Coe a gourd dipper full. He took the dipper and started to drink and just as he did he got his first full view of the woman's face, which had been hidden by the split bonnet. Her mouth was ringed with snuff and snuffy saliva was dripping off her chin.

He looked at the rim of the gourd dipper and saw brown stains. He didn't want to drink it but he knew he had to. He had been noticing that the water was leaking in a steady stream from the end of the handle when he upended it, and it occurred to him, brilliantly, he thought, that that was the solution, to drink out of the end of the handle. And he did. When he finished draining the dipper gourd, the woman laughed and said, "I'll swanny, you're the only one I ever saw who drinks from that gourd just like I do."

Just before the pair left, Stanley asked the woman what time it was. "Wait a minnit, and I'll go inside and see."

She went to the door leading into the kitchen and looked at the strips of sunlight on the floor and came back.

"Hit's two cracks till twelve," she said.

The Big Thicket is the most fascinating place I have ever known —and I have explored almost all of the Yellow House and Palo

31

Duro canyons, followed the Canadian River, the Pease River, the Salt Fork of the Red River, and Prairie Dog Town Creek from their beginnings to their ends.

About six years ago, I published a picture of the ivory-billed woodpecker in *The Kountze News*, saying that it was extinct over all the nation except possibly in the Big Thicket, and that there might be a few left in the deep recesses of the tight-eye Thicket.

About a month later, a native of the Thicket came into the *News* printing shop carrying a dead woodpecker.

"Ain't this the bird you said was extinct?" he asked.

At once I thought it was, but did not say so, and hunted up all the pictures and descriptions I had of the ivory-billed woodpecker, and I read the detailed description to the hunter. As I read he checked off each identifying point on the dead bird.

"Hit's hit all right," he said. "I studied this particular wood-pecker for a week before I shot one. I got in real clost. I can't read, but I had my boy read that what you put in the paper 'bout the woodpecker, every night. I memorized hit. I killed hit because I knew you wouldn't believe me unless I tuck hit to you."

My face must have revealed my utter despair, frustration, and sadness. He looked at me intently and finally grinned.

"You needn't feel so bad about me killing this un. There's a whole lot more where I got him. But I ain't goin' to tell nobody. Not even the feller from A&M; and I ain't going to tell you where hit is. In fact, I'm goin' to take this bird back with me. If I've got all them extinct woodpeckers, I'll be the most important man in the world, even if nobody knows hit but me, and that's the way I want hit."

# TALES OF THE
# ALABAMA-COUSHATTA INDIANS*

BY HOWARD N. MARTIN

*There is not much left in the Big Thicket to tell us about the first men who hunted in its woods. At least ten thousand years ago hunters left their spear heads in East Texas in the remains of sloths and mastodons and other now-extinct animals, but so far nothing has been found to show that these early Americans roamed or settled in the Thicket area.*

*Three groups of Indians are historically associated with the Thicket. They are the Atakapans, the Caddoes, and the Alabama-Coushatta. In the historical beginning, however, only the Atakapan and the Caddo moved through the Thicket with any regularity. Other tribes from as far away as Oklahoma, Colorado, and Kansas made periodic hunting trips into the Thicket for bear meat, skins, and tallow; and Tonkawas, Lipans, and Wichitas met in peace at the medicinal springs around present-day Sour Lake and Saratoga. But primarily the Thicket was the meat house of the mound-building Caddoes, who occupied the fertile rolling hills to the north, and the cannibalistic Atakapans, who bounded the Thicket on the Gulf Coast and on the Trinity bottoms. Then at the end of the eighteenth century, the Alabama and Coushatta began*

17. Howard N. Martin.

*to settle on the northern and western fringe of the Thicket, and the woods became theirs.*

*Howard N. Martin's collection of "Tales of the Alabama-Coushatta Indians" is selected from his unpublished history of the two tribes and from his* FOLKTALES OF THE ALABAMA-COUSHATTA INDIANS. *Mr. Martin's research on these East Texas Indians will undoubtedly be the basis for a definitive work on the only tribes of Indians left in Texas.—F.E.A.*

### The Trail West for the Alabama Indian Tribe

A small group of armed settlers moved quietly across the prairie to form a tight circle around an Indian camp on the Lower Brazos Reserve in Central Texas. Clouds obscured the moon and accentuated the darkness of that December night in 1858.

In the distance a coyote howled. But in the Indian camp there was no sound or movement among the Anadarko and Caddo men, women, and children. No one stood guard while the seventeen Indians slept.

After the Texans had taken positions around the Indians, the leader rose to a standing position and began firing a shotgun into the camp. The other men also opened fire. At point-blank range the blazing rifles took frightful toll. Seven of the Indians were killed instantly; most of the others were seriously wounded.

Indian Agent Robert S. Neighbors immediately appealed to Governor Runnels for prompt action against the murderers of these peaceful Indians. The agent pointed out that these Indians had harmed no one and were the innocent victims of vengeful white settlers.

Details of this event must be recorded among the more tragic incidents in the history of this state's relations with its Indian population. The misfortune of the Anadarko and Caddo Indians on this occasion, however, proved to be a lucky break for the Alabama Indian Tribe located then, as now, on a reservation in Polk County, Texas.

The Alabama tribe was a proud but peaceful member of the Upper Creek Confederacy. When the French began establishing posts along the Gulf of Mexico in the eighteenth century, they found the Alabamas living in several villages on the Alabama River where the Coosa and Tallapoosa rivers meet. The state of Alabama and the Alabama River are named for these Indians.

The French built Fort Toulouse at this river junction. Although they were at war with the Alabamas from 1702 until 1713, the French later maintained friendly relations with them and other nearby tribes. They also convinced these Indians that the English were enemies. So, when the French abandoned Fort Toulouse and Mobile to the English in 1763, most of the Alabamas destroyed their villages and followed the French to Louisiana. Some settled along the Mississippi and Red rivers, while the majority drifted westward to build a village near Opelousas.

By 1800 the Alabamas had begun moving across the border into

## Map 2. INDIAN VILLAGE SITES AND INDIAN TRAILS.

(White numbers on black background refer to village sites. Villages numbered 1 through 8 existed prior to 1835; numbers 9 through 11 were established after 1835.)

1. Peachtree Village
2. Flea Village
3. Fenced-in Village
4. Battise Village
5. Long King's Village
6. Colita's Village
7. Campground (probably used by both Alabamas and Coushattas)
8. Village of the Pacana Muscogies (Creeks) on the John Burgess League
9. Barclay Village
10. Rock Village
11. Alabama-Coushatta Reservation; consists of 1,110.7 acres granted by the state of Texas to the Alabama Tribe in 1854 and 3,071 acres purchased by the federal government in 1928 for the Alabama and Coushatta tribes.

(Black numbers on white background indicate towns and communities. These are shown as geographical reference points. All except Fort Teran were established after 1835.)

12. Fort Teran
13. Livingston
14. Moscow
15. Woodville
16. Smithville
17. Swarthout
18. Onalaska
19. Goodrich

(Black letters on white background indicate trails that existed prior to 1835.)

A. Coushatta Trace—from a Coushatta village on the Sabine River to the Colorado River south of Columbus
B. Long King's Trace—from Peachtree Village to a point near the western boundary of San Jacinto County, where this trail merged with the Coushatta Trace
C. Alabama Trace—from the San Antonio Road east of Nacogdoches through Peachtree Village and the site of the present Alabama-Coushatta Reservation to Colita's Village on the Trinity River
D. Liberty-Nacogdoches Road—originally used by the Spanish in trips between Nacogdoches and the mouth of the Trinity River; later extensively used by the Alabamas and Coushattas
E. Kickapoo Trace—from the Battise Village on the Trinity River to the Kickapoo Indian Village near Palestine
F. Battise Trace—from the Battise Village to Long King's Village
G. Colita's Trace—from Colita's Village to Long King's Village
H. Long Tom's Trace—from Long King's Village to the Long Tom Creek area
I. Campground Trace—from Long King's Village to the campground south of the present Alabama-Coushatta Reservation

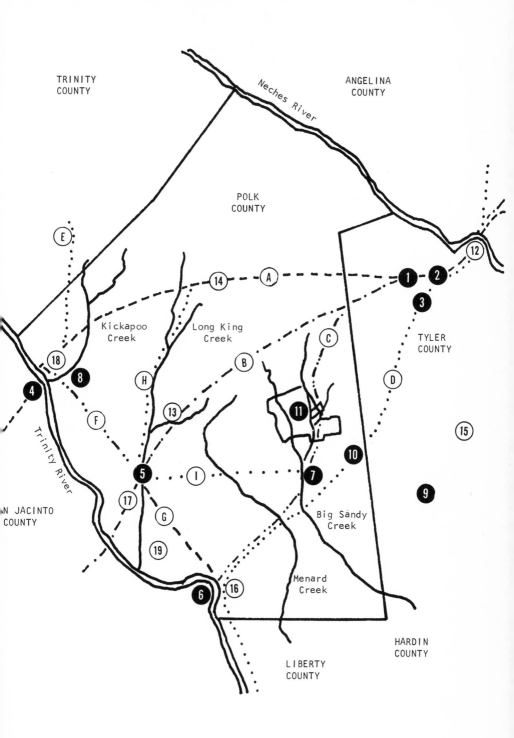

TRINITY
COUNTY

ANGELINA
COUNTY

Neches River

POLK
COUNTY

E

14   A   1   2

12

3

Kickapoo
Creek

Long King
Creek

C

TYLER
COUNTY

18

B

D

H

4

8

11

15

F

13

10

Trinity River

5

I

7

N JACINTO
COUNTY

17

G

9

Big Sandy
Creek

19

16

Menard
Creek

6

HARDIN
COUNTY

LIBERTY
COUNTY

18. Chief Charles Martin Thompson (he died in 1935)
of the Alabama-Coushattas (Courtesy H. N. Martin).

Spanish Texas. Here the Indians found a welcome, since the Spanish considered Texas to be the outer fortress that stood guard against first the French and then, after 1803, the Americans. From the Spanish viewpoint, the maintenance of this Texas defense line depended substantially upon the loyal service of the friendly Indian tribes between the Trinity and Sabine rivers. Accordingly, Spain appropriated large sums of money to buy clothing, medals, guns, knives, and other types of gifts for the Indians. These items were given to the Indians who visited Nacogdoches.

Dr. John Sibley, the American agent in Nachitoches, Louisiana, also realized the importance of influencing the border Indians. His trading post was a popular gathering point for the Indians in the area. Here the Alabamas and other tribes received gifts and expressed loyalty to the Americans. Then, at the first opportunity, they would travel to Nacogdoches for Spanish gifts and friendship. The Alabamas apparently understood that the Spanish and Americans were engaged in a tug-of-war for their loyalty, and the Indians capitalized on this conflict in accordance with the opportunities that came their way.

By 1805 the Alabamas had established a village on the Angelina River. They also built homes at various sites along the Neches River, and in 1830 these Indians were living in three villages at the intersection of the Coushatta Trace and the Liberty-Nacogdoches Road in northwestern Tyler County.

During the Texas War for Independence the Alabamas remained neutral, according to a tradition that is still known among the Indians now living on the Alabama-Coushatta Reservation. Many moved to the Opelousas district of Louisiana until the end of the war. Those who remained in Texas fed the white settlers who passed through the Alabama villages in the "Runaway Scrape."

In 1840 the Republic of Texas Congress granted the Alabamas two leagues of land which included the Fenced-in Village in northwestern Tyler County. When the surveyors came to survey this land, the Indians, thinking the grant was for the whites, departed for Louisiana, leaving their hogs, cattle, and two hundred acres of fenced-in land suitable for cultivation.

The Alabamas returned from Louisiana a few months later and found white settlers in possession of their land. Consequently, the Indians drifted southward and formed a village on land owned by James Barclay on Horse Pen Creek in Tyler County. Later the Alabamas established the Rock Village, located on the Liberty-Nacogdoches Road about five miles east of the present reservation.

In 1854 the state of Texas purchased 1,110.7 acres of heavily timbered land in Polk County as a reservation for the Alabamas. Title to this land is vested in the tribe and is tax free and inalienable. The Alabamas settled on this land in 1855.

In their century-long search for lands free from the white man's intrusion, the Alabamas had to choose between the use of force or the use of peaceful means to secure homesites. No doubt the Alabamas could have mustered a relatively substantial military force in the first half of the nineteenth century and would have fought when necessary. They proved their valor as warriors not only in early battles with the French (1702–1713) but later—in World War II and in Korea.

The Alabamas as a tribe refused to use force against the white settlers. They chose, instead, to exercise patience, restraint, and diplomacy in relations with their neighbors. When white settlers drove off their stock and devastated their fields, they did not retaliate. Chief Antone and Sub-Chief Sylestine would appeal to General Sam Houston and other influential friends for protection. While some of the other Texas tribes used force to defend their lands, the Alabamas wrote memorials and petitions to appropriate governing authorities to call attention to their needs and to request land for reservations.

In 1858 the state of Texas attempted to move the Alabamas to a new Indian reservation along the Brazos River in Central Texas. James Barclay, state agent for the Alabamas, rode across Texas on horseback in October of that year with Chief Antone and Sub-Chief Sylestine of the Alabamas and Chiefs Mingo and Chickasaw Abbey of the Coushattas, to inspect the new reservation. From the Indians' viewpoint, the Lower Brazos Reserve was a dark, dreary land compared to the forested hills of their Polk County reservation. The Indian leaders told Agent Barclay that they did not want to move from East Texas.

In December of 1858 Governor Runnels received the news of the shooting of the Anadarko and Caddo Indians on the Lower Brazos Reserve. The governor's reaction to this event is expressed in his letter to James Barclay, in which he stated that he had abandoned his plan to move the Alabamas and Coushattas to the Lower Brazos Reserve: "charity and humanity forbid it under present circum-

19. Bronson Cooper Sylestine, current chief of the Alabama-Coushattas (Courtesy H. N. Martin).

stances; my own conscience revolts at the idea of practising a deception upon the Indians, or carrying them where they might at any time be indiscriminately slaughtered, for no other cause than that the Creator has made them Indians . . ."

Thus, reaction to the murder of the peaceful Anadarko and Caddo Indians in 1858 was a significant factor in blocking this final attempt by the state of Texas to move the Alabamas from their Polk County reservation. The trail west for the Alabamas ended in the Big Thicket of East Texas.

## Coushatta Pawns of the Texas Colonists

The morning sun revealed two opposing armies in battle formation nine miles southeast of San Antonio on March 29, 1813. Spain's red and gold banner waved above fifteen hundred regulars and one thousand militiamen arrayed on a wooded slope.

A half mile in front of the Spaniards, thirteen hundred Gutiérrez-Magee filibusters, commanded by Samuel Kemper, waited the signal to charge. Twenty-five Coushatta Indians crouched in front of this army's right flank.

Units of Kemper's army passed the word that a low tapping on a drum would signal the attack. But these instructions confused the Coushattas. Suddenly, the Coushattas shocked both armies with a wild charge up the hill toward the Spanish line. All other units held fast, waiting for the signal drum. At the drum tap, the whole line moved forward with such cool precision that the frightened Spaniards broke ranks and fled toward San Antonio. The Battle of Rosalis (or Salado) ended in victory for Kemper's republican army.

In their lonely charge against the Spanish in 1813, the Coushattas proved their loyalty to the early colonists in Texas. Beginning with the Battle of Rosalis the Coushatta tribe wrote an unbroken record of faithful service to Texas. Ironically, they were repaid with nothing: broken promises were the only response to their requests for small tracts of land to be used as permanent Texas homes.

The Coushatta Indian Tribe was a member of the Upper Creek

Confederacy and has always been closely associated with the Alabama Tribe. Many of the Coushattas who lived near the Alabamas around Fort Toulouse accompanied the latter on their migration in 1763 from their homes on the Alabama River to Louisiana. Of several villages that the Coushattas established in various sections of Louisiana, the largest was located near the mouth of Quicksand Creek on the Sabine River.

For nearly a century after 1763 the Coushattas were forced to move from one place to another in search of permanent homes. If white men wanted the land on which the Coushattas happened to be living, the Coushattas moved.

By 1800 the Coushattas were drifting across the border into Spanish Texas. The Indians were welcomed by the Spanish officials who expected them to strengthen the wall of friendly tribes which bulwarked Texas' eastern border.

During the early nineteenth century, Coushattas blazed a vital trail from the Sabine River west to La Bahía. This trail—the Coushatta Trace—was a wilderness thoroughfare for Indians, smugglers, and adventurers traveling between Mexico and Louisiana.

To control this traffic through the heart of Texas the Spanish posted Coushattas at strategic points on the Trinity River to serve as sentinels and scouts. Their assignment: inform the Spanish in Nacogdoches of any movement along the Coushatta Trace or on the Trinity River.

The Upper Coushatta Village (Battise) stood where the Coushatta Trace crossed the Trinity. Long King's Village, the middle village, was on Long King Creek, about four miles north of the Trinity. In the Lower Coushatta Village lived Colita, one of the best-known Indian leaders in East Texas. This village, in San Jacinto County, stood at the "shirt-tail bend" of the Trinity.

In 1830 the Coushattas reached the zenith of their existence in independent villages. About six hundred lived in or near the three Coushatta communities. They farmed, hunted, and traded with white settlers.

During the Texas War for Independence against Mexico, the

Coushattas remained neutral at General Sam Houston's request. But they fed and cared for white settlers who surged through the Coushatta villages in the "Runaway Scrape," when Texas families fled before Santa Anna's advancing Mexican Army prior to the Battle of San Jacinto.

The year 1840 found the Coushattas on the move again. White settlers were claiming their village sites, and village life started to disintegrate.

Prospects brightened briefly when the Republic of Texas Congress in 1840 granted two leagues of land to the Coushattas for permanent reservations. The land was surveyed and the field notes were filed. But the grants never became effective—white settlers had already claimed the land.

By 1845, the year that the Republic of Texas became the twenty-eighth state of the United States, the former inhabitants of Long King's Village and the Battise Village were forced to wander around Polk County forests or join the Coushattas remaining at Colita's Village. Colonel Hamilton Washington had purchased Colita's village site but permitted the Indians to remain on the land.

Two events in the early 1850's lengthened the dark shadows over Coushatta prospects. The first disaster was the death of Chief Colita in 1852. He had given the Coushattas such effective leadership that the *Galveston News* editorially lamented his death. Thus, the tribe was left leaderless at a crucial moment in its history.

In 1855 the Texas legislature granted the Coushattas 640 acres of land for a reservation. But because suitable open land was no longer available in Polk County, this grant remained only a scrap of paper.

Fortunately for the Coushattas, their kinsmen, the Alabama Indian Tribe had received a grant of land in 1854. With the permission of the Alabamas, most of the Coushattas settled on this reservation in 1859. A few remained on the Hamilton Washington plantation until 1906, when they joined the others in Polk County.

The Polk County reservation was increased to 4,181.7 acres in 1928 when the United States Congress purchased an additional 3,071 acres of adjoining land. The deed was issued to the Alabama and Coushatta Indian Tribes, and the name "Alabama-Coushatta" has been used since 1928 as the official title of this enlarged reservation. Today, nearly four hundred Alabamas and Coushattas live in the security of this land.

After years of struggle along a heartbreaking trail that wound from Alabama to East Texas, the Coushattas found a permanent home in the hills of Polk County. Here they would no longer need to dread the surveying crews, coming to stake their village sites as homes for white settlers. At home at last, they would no longer be pushed around at the white man's pleasure, like pawns on an East Texas chessboard.

## The Creation of the Earth†

In the beginning everything was covered by water. The only living things were a few small animals who occupied a raft floating about on the water. Nothing else could be seen above the surface of the water.

One day the animals decided that they wanted to make the land appear; so they called for a volunteer to make the attempt. Crawfish volunteered, and he dived off the raft. The water was so deep, however, that he was unable to reach the BOTTOM of the great ocean.

Three days later Crawfish again tried to reach the bottom, but again he failed. On the third trial, though, he reached the bottom. Using his tail to scoop up the mud, Crawfish worked rapidly and built a mound higher and higher. Soon the top of the mud chimney stuck up above the surface of the water. Then the mud began spreading to all sides. In this manner it formed a great mass of soft earth.

The animals looked in all directions. They agreed that Crawfish had done a good job, but they thought that the surface of the earth was too smooth. So Buzzard was sent out to shape the earth's surface. Now Buzzard was a huge bird with long, powerful wings. He

†The following legends were taken from Mr. Martin's book, *Folktales of the Alabama-Coushatta Indians* (Livingston, Texas: Polk County Historical Association, 1946).

flew along just above the top of the soft earth, flapping his wings. When his wings swung down, they cut deep holes or valleys in the soft earth. When his wings swung up, they formed the hills and mountains. When Buzzard didn't flap his wings and just sailed along, he made the level country or plains. And so the surface of the earth is made up of plains, valleys, and mountains.

### The Origin of the Alabama-Coushatta Indians

Indians were made from clay down in a big cave under the earth. They lived in this cave a long time before some of them decided to go up to the surface of the earth. After they started upward, they camped three times on the way. Finally, at noon on the fourth day, they reached the mouth of the cave.

The Indians found that a large tree was standing in the mouth of the cave. The Alabamas and the Coushattas went out of the cave on opposite sides of a root of this big tree. Thus, these two tribes differed somewhat in speech, but they have always lived near each other.

At first the Indians would stay outside only during the night, returning to the cave when day came. One night when the Indians came out of the cave to play, they heard an owl hooting. Most of the Indians became to scared that they ran back into the cave and never returned to the surface of the earth. That is why the Alabamas and Coushattas are so few. If the owl had not hooted, then all the Indians would have remained on the surface of the earth, and the Alabamas and Coushattas would have been more numerous.

One day a white man came to the cave and saw some tracks in the sand. He wanted to find out who had made the tracks, so he went to the place three times but did not see anyone. He finally decided to play a trick on these strange people. Early one morning he put a barrel of whiskey near the place where he found the footprints. When the Indians came out of the cave that night to play, they saw the barrel and wondered what was in it. One of the men became so curious that he tasted the contents and soon he began to feel good and to sing and dance. Then the others drank also and

20. Cemetery at the Alabama-Coushatta Reservation.

21. Cemetery at the Alabama-Coushatta Reservation.

became so drunk that the white man was able to catch them. After that the Alabamas and Coushattas had to stay on top of the earth and were not allowed to go near the big cave.

## The Great Flood

One day an Indian rescued a frog from a fire. After the frog's burns had been healed, the grateful creature said to his Indian friend, "Within a short while the land will disappear beneath the water. Make a raft and put a thick layer of grass underneath so the beavers can not cut holes in the logs."

The Indian was alarmed by the warning, so he got some long dry logs and tied them together. He put some grass underneath so the beavers couldn't cut the logs. The Indian warned the other members of the tribe that a great flood would cover the land. But everyone just laughed at Frog's prediction and made fun of the Indian who was crazy enough to build such a huge raft far from deep water. Their laughter was cut short, though, for soon the great flood came. The builder of the raft then assembled his family, Frog, and many other creatures on the clumsy boat. Higher and higher rose the water. The birds flew up to the sky and caught hold of it. Soon all living things except the birds and the creatures on the raft were drowned.

Woodpecker got so close to the sun that his head was burned. That's why his feathers turned red. Since that time this bird has been called the red-headed woodpecker.

One bird with a long tail caught hold of the sky, but the water rose so high that its feathers became wet, causing the tail feathers to divide and curl slightly. This bird was called the scissor-tail.

## The Origin of Corn and Tobacco

In a certain Indian village lived six brothers, known among the tribe as great hunters. When their supply of food would run short, one or more of the brothers would go hunting, and seldom did they return without an abundance of meat. During one such hunting trip, the youngest brother made camp at a place near which two strange men had already built a fire. The next morning the two men called to the young Indian, "Come and eat with us."

When the meal was finished, the grateful young man then volunteered to take care of the camp while his two hosts went hunting. After they had gone, the Indian snapped his fingers against a little clay pot which started growing larger. Into the pot he put food and water, and kept up a fire beneath until it boiled. Although the young Indian wanted to help his friends, they seemed to be sad when they saw the dinner he had prepared. One of them said, "Everything is spoiled for us. We are spirits and cannot eat boiled food. Now we must leave you."

Before leaving, though, the strangers went bear hunting with the young Indian. The trail of a bear was found, and the three set out to tree the bear. For three days they followed the bear and on the fourth day they made a discovery that turned the young Indian's attention from the bear hunt. He found two red kernels which the strangers said were kernels of corn. Farther down the trail the Indian found two other kernels of corn, which he picked up and carried with him. Again the Indian found several kernels in the path, and again he picked them up and carried them with him. Presently the trail of corn kernels ended, and there in front of them was a large field of ripe corn. The men said, "You must stay here," and they showed him how to make corncribs. Next, they gave him some tobacco seed and instructed him to plant it and smoke the leaves of the tobacco plants. Then the two strangers disappeared since they had completed their mission to carry corn and tobacco to the Indians.

### Why Fire Came to the Indians

For a long time Fire was in the custody of the Bears, who guarded it very closely and even took it about with them. No creature except a member of the Bear clan was allowed to use Fire or even to approach it.

One day the Bears put Fire on the ground and went away to eat acorns. Now Fire had to have a lot of attention. Since the Bears didn't come back that day, Fire was slowly dying and began calling for help. But the Bears had traveled so far into the woods that they couldn't hear Fire's calls. Some Indians heard him, though, and hurried to his aid. They got a stick from the north and laid it on Fire. In the west they found another stick and fed it to Fire. The third stick laid on the flame they brought from the south. Then they went to the east for another stick. When it was laid down, Fire blazed up.

After the Bears had finished their meal of acorns, they returned to claim Fire; however, Fire said, "I don't Know the Bears any longer." Thus, Fire left the Bears and went to live with the Indians.

### Abba Mingo's Son and the Corn-Grinder

Abba Mingo, the great chief of the earth and sky, was very sad. Some of his people on earth were quarreling. Abba Mingo was puzzled. He called a council of the wisest men and asked them what to do. Many pipes were smoked before a word was spoken. Finally, the oldest man said, "Send Abba Mingo's son to earth." Then Abba Mingo's son picked up a peace pipe and went down to earth.

When he reached a village, some bad Indians started plotting against him. They caught him and although they wished him dead, they were afraid to kill him. It happened that a blind corngrinder lived in this village. So they sent for the old corngrinder and seated him in the council circle. The bad Indians placed the point of a spear against the side of Abba Mingo's son, who was tied to a tree. Into the hands of the corngrinder they placed the handle of the spear and told him to push. He did so and unwittingly killed Abba Mingo's son, who remained standing, to the amazement of the spectators. Some of the blood of the dead visitor fell on the eyes of the blind corngrinder and his sight was immediately restored. When the corngrinder saw what he had done, he died, but he too remained standing.

Then an even greater miracle occurred. There seemed to be two strangers and two corngrinders. The two newcomers were the spirits of the two dead men. Then the spirit of Abba Mingo's son led the spirit of the corngrinder to a beautiful country far above the earth.

### The Westward Migration of the Alabamas

During the early years the Alabama Indians lived upon acorns and cane sprouts. Later they made bows and arrows to kill deer; and used sharp rocks to cut up the meat. To kindle a fire they used as a drill the stem of a weed called *hassala'po* (plant-with-which-to-make-fire), which is like sassafras, and the wood of a tree called *baksa* (bass) for a base stick.

They built their village near a large river and stayed there a long time. Presently they came in contact with the Choctaw and warred against them, almost destroying one Choctaw town. So the Choctaw became disheartened and wanted to make peace. For this purpose the Choctaw selected a poor man, to whom they promised to give two girls if he were successful in his peace mission. Then they gave him a white deerskin shirt, white deerskin leggings, and moccasins. Next, they put several strings of white beads about his neck and a rattle in his hand.

Thus provided, the Choctaw peace emissary crossed to the first Alabama village shaking his rattle and singing as he went. When the Alabamas heard him, they came out, took hold of him and accompanied him to the village. When they came near the town, they raised the Choctaw on their backs and entered the place in this manner, singing continuously. Then they set him down, and he talked to them for a long time, laying down one string of white beads as he did so. Then he set out for another Alabama village, accompanied as before. At the second village he made another long talk and laid out a second string of white beads. He did the same at the third village. This was the end of his peace mission, and he therefore returned to the Choctaw, who gave him the girls as they had promised.

One summer an Alabama said he wanted to go west, and several wished to go with him, but a berdache (half-man) tried to stop him. "Why are you going?" he asked.

To this question the Alabama replied, "I am going in order to kill turkey, deer, and other animals; after that I will return."

"There are plenty of turkey and deer here," said the berdache. But the Alabama still wanted to go, and after they had argued for some time the berdache said, "You are a man, but you want to run away. I will not run. I will not run, although my grandfather used to say that the English and French are all hard fighters. When they come, I will take my knife, lie down under the bed, and keep striking at them until they kill me."

Nevertheless, the Alabama and his friends started off. They came to a river, made canoes, and proceeded along it a great distance until they finally reached a Choctaw settlement. They stopped for a while, thinking that these people were friends. Presently, though, the Alabamas observed that the Choctaws were making arrows. So the Alabamas got into their canoes and continued down the river.

By and by they came upon many bears swimming in the river, and some wanted to kill them, but others said, "Don't shoot," and they kept on. Later they heard noises behind them, and one of the man said, "People are following us." A short distance ahead many canes were observed growing in the mouth of a creek which flowed into the river, so they shoved their canoes into this canebrake and waited. After a while they heard the Choctaw canoes pass, but the Alabamas decided to stay in the canebrake all that night. Just before the sun came up, they heard the sounds of the Choctaw war party again. Not until the Choctaws went by and disappeared up the river did the Alabamas dare to continue their journey.

A few days later the travelers arrived at the house of a white man. He exchanged corn for venison and told them that the route by the river which they had intended to take was very long and that he knew a shorter way. So he tied oxen to their canoes and dragged them across a narrow place to another river.

Farther down this river they stopped at a trading post belonging to a white blacksmith. From him the Indians got knives and axes in exchange for venison. Some Choctaws living nearby said to them, "There is no war here. There is peace. We are friends of the

Alabamas." Afterward, however, some of both tribes got drunk on whiskey bought at the store and wanted to fight. But the Alabamas who had stayed sober took their people down to the canoes, put them in, and started along.

After leaving the blacksmith, the Alabamas went to Bayou Boeuf. Later they moved to Opelousas, Louisiana, and still later to Tyler County, Texas. Next, they settled Peachtree Village. There were many Alabamas at that time, and they separated into a number of villages. One was north of North Woodville and was called Cane Island, because a lot of canes were found along a nearby creek. They were living in these towns when the war between Texas and Mexico broke out.

General Houston had visited the Alabamas and asked them not to fight with either side during the war. Therefore, the Alabamas remained neutral, and many went back to Louisiana, leaving only a few in Peachtree Village. To show that they were neutral, the Alabamas who stayed in the village hung up a large piece of white cloth every time a group of fleeing Texans approached the village. Some of the whites who passed through Peachtree Village were almost perishing with hunger and were given food and drink by the Alabamas.

After the white people had left the region, the Mexicans went to a town on a big river, and the soldiers opened the abandoned stores and used the goods. Some of the soldiers wanted to cross the big river near the town and threw bales of cotton into the water to form a temporary bridge. After the Mexicans had crossed the river, they drove away some Indians who were camping nearby.

From a distant place some white men came to fight the Mexicans. Several of the whites went around the town and broke down a bridge over a bad creek so the Mexicans couldn't escape in that direction. Then a big fight started. Many guns were fired. Of all the Mexican soldiers who took part in the battle, only their General Santa Anna and a few others got away. The general fell down in a thicket. While he was in the thicket, two deer whistled, indicating to the whites where Santa Anna was hiding. The latter was captured and taken to the camp of the whites. After the Mexican general had agreed to give up all the land in this country and had promised not to bother the white people any more, he was allowed to get into a boat and sail away.

## Chief Colita of the Coushatta Indians

In the year 1834 a number of colonists made their way into that section of Texas now known as San Jacinto County. On the morning of April 18, 1836, a messenger came to the settlements in this region and advised the colonists of the approach of the Mexican Army under Santa Anna. No sooner had the messenger continued his journey to the other settlements than refugees from the more southerly villages began to pass in haste to avoid the oncoming devastation.

The waters of the Trinity seemed to offer refuge to the frightened Texans, as, once across the river, they felt that they would have placed a barrier between them and the Napoleon of the West. Immediately the San Jacinto settlers made ready to join the "Runaway Scrape," and long before nightfall they were well on their way. Some were in wagons others on horseback, and many of the less fortunate were forced to travel on foot.

When the Trinity River was reached, the refugees found that the ferryboat had been washed away! The April showers had proved to be torrents, and the usually peaceful stream was a wide and muddy barrier between the Texans and the territory which they considered as a haven. But more threatening than the murky Trinity were some Indians who appeared on the opposite bank. Despair must have rushed with a mighty surge over the weary and wet pioneers as they faced apparent annihilation at the hands of the Indians. Could it be the Cherokees on march to join Santa Anna? Was it a band sent by the Mexicans to cut them off before they reached Louisiana? These and countless other thoughts must have caught at the throats of the bewildered mothers as they pressed their babies closer to their breasts. Every man held his gun cautiously but surely. Through the dim haze which enveloped the river and the misty rain which was falling, the group of Indians could be seen gathered near the ferry landing on the opposite side of the river. The colonists thought that in a few minutes the Indians would attack them. Retreat was impossible. The heavy, rich black land of the bottoms was a veritable mire. All afternoon they had labored from one bog to another with the wagons, and now they were completely fatigued. Time would not pass. The Indians on the opposite bank seemed as still as the nearby oak and pecan trees.

Suddenly a lone Indian reined his horse down the bank to the water, hesitated, and then plunged in. Would the others follow? Halfway across the muddy, rolling water the rider held forth his hand and boomed a friendly greeting. It was Colita, chief of the friendly Coushattas, riding his famous horse! For a swift second the refugees were speechless. Then the woods rang with their shouts of rejoicing.

The refugees advised Colita of their plight and of the approach of the Mexicans. At a signal from their chief the Coushattas turned their horses into the river and quickly made the other bank. Trees were felled and fastened to the sides of the wagons to convert them into improvised rafts, and in a few hours the Texans, tired, wet, and famished, were safe on the north bank of the Trinity.

The Coushatta women gathered from the nearby hunting village. Fires were made and meat put into large clay pots to boil. They had an abundance of meat ready to cook, because General Houston had asked them to be prepared to help the refugees as they fled eastward. Some of the colonists were so hungry that they did not wait until the meat was cooked; instead, they ate chunks of raw beef.

While the hungry whites ate the hasty meal and warmed their hearts in this new-found hospitality, a scream broke from a startled and delirious mother. In the frenzy of guarding her nine children in the hazardous crossing of the river, she had left one of her babies asleep in a dismantled wagon on the other side. Chief Colita caught her almost incoherent words and again forced his horse across the rolling waters. He quickly returned holding the crying baby above his head and placed her in her mother's arms.

When the meal was finished, a few of the leaders of the colonists held council with Colita. Indian country still lay between them and Louisiana, and rumor had it that several Indian tribes, influenced by Mexican agents, would pillage the East Texas settlements at any moment. But Colita was mindful of these dangers and soon relieved the anxiety of the whites. In keeping with his pledge to General Houston to help protect the white people against such raids, Colita dispatched a strong guard of his warriors to accompany the Texans to the Louisiana border.

Four days after the harrowing crossing of the Trinity the band of refugees, now greatly enlarged by other settlers fleeing from the common danger, were surprised by the approach of a group of men from the rear. It was Colita and a few of his men coming to bring them the news of the victory at San Jacinto. In scant English Colita told the news as it had been given to him by the runner sent by Houston with the admonition that it be taken as quickly as possible to the settlers who had been forced to leave their homes.

# SETTLING THE OLD POPLAR-TREE PLACE

BY VINSON ALLEN COLLINS

*Pioneer life has always been much the same; a family pulls up stakes in the home town and sets out for a new life in a new country, where they will be on their own. A lot of the Big Thicket settlers followed that pattern pretty well. Whether they were getting away from something or were looking for something, what they found was big timber and privacy and the chance to prove to themselves that they could be independent.*

*There weren't many towns near the Thicket when the Collins and Hooks and Harts began coming in during the 'forties and 'fifties. There were a few stores in Old Hardin, near present-day Kountze, and there were settlements at Woodville, and at Concord (the steamboat landing on Pine Island Bayou) and at Drews Landing on the Trinity, but these places were a long way off for most of the settlers. However, the old nesters that came to get some privacy in the Thicket weren't interested in spending much time in town. They liked the lonesome and they wanted to be apart so they could look after themselves.*

*Warren Collins and his family came to the Big Thicket in 1852 from Mississippi. They brought along some poplar tree sprouts in gourds and set them out at their homestead near Honey Island. By one of those miracles of life, the seedlings lived and grew into trees,*

22. Vinson A. Collins.

and the old home place was known thereafter as the Old Poplar-Tree Place.

Warren Collins was a short, square-set, long-armed, and hammer-fisted sort of man, who ruled his roost and was a power among his clan and neighbors. He fought anything that had the gall to cross him and was the leader of the Jayhawkers during the Civil War. His mind was set as hard as his fists and he didn't reckon that the war between the North and South was any part of his plan of life. He had come to the Thicket in the first place to get away from just that sort of foolishness.

Warren Collins was what Robert Burns would call "the man of independent mind," and the customs of his home reflect just that. He was his own man and what he couldn't hunt and gather, the family did without. Warren's son, the Honorable V. A. Collins, wrote the following description of his family life in the Big Thicket *as it was during the middle of the nineteenth century. "Uncle Yank," as Senator Collins is called, profited largely by his father's independent example and led as fruitful a life in Texas politics as his father did in the Big Thicket.*

*With Mr. Collins' permission, I have edited his article from his history of Hardin County (contained in Mrs. W. J. Norvell's history of the Pitts family), his own family history, and a personal letter. He wrote most of what follows in 1962, when he was ninety-five years old.—F.E.A.*

It was said to be about five hundred miles from Jones County, Mississippi, to Hardin County, Texas, and they had to make this trip in ox wagons. Stacey Collins, Jr., had a wagon and a yoke of oxen to carry his family, and Stacey, Sr., and Sara Anderson Collins went with their three sons, Newton, Warren, and Edwin, in another wagon. I think it took about twenty-five days for them to make the trip from Mississippi to Hardin County.

Uncle Edwin heard that there were no poplar trees in Texas, so he decided to take some along and plant them. He was told that the trip would take so long that the little trees would probably die before they arrived, so he said he would plant two little poplars in gourds and let them take root before they started, and then he would take them along with him in the wagon. This he did.

There was no lumber to build regular houses from at that time, but there were millions of pine saplings just the right size to make log houses out of, with the poles notched and laid on each other and then roofed with boards split out of large pines. That would build a very good summer house, but to keep out the cold wind in the winter they had to cut large pines and rive out sealing boards with a froe. They would cover each one of the cracks between the logs with a sealing board, and those boards were of considerable length—eight or ten feet long. When they got the sealing boards nailed, they had a very comfortable house. To make it liveable they

23. A pre-Civil War log house.

had to have a chimney at one end of the house. The chimney was
made by splitting chimney sticks, digging clay out of the ground
and mixing it with water, and putting that clay all around the
chimney sticks; they tapered the chimney as it went up so as to
make it draw smoke.

One of the first essentials in a new settlement was to prepare a little farm and raise some corn. The only bread these people had at that time was cornbread. My folks cleared a farm very early, and the land being new and fresh, it was productive; ten acres planted in corn would yield all that any family needed during a year.

In the country, where people farmed and cleared land for that purpose, it took several years to rid the farm of all timber, and it was a glorious old custom for neighbors to go several miles to meet other neighbors and roll logs. Not always, but very often when the men rolled logs, the women would gather at the same house and quilt a quilt. While this was a day of labor, yet it was a holiday. There was no other day in the year that meant so much to country folks as log-rolling day. The best food ever tasted was served; the most brilliant feast of the gods could not excel a log-rolling dinner, and an abundance was left over for supper.

Supper being over, the quilt being detached from the frames, and the frames being removed from the room, some old country fiddler would begin to tune up his fiddle and rosin up his bow, and then he would pull the horse's tail across the cat guts, and the red russet shoes would begin to "come and tip it as they go, on the light fantastic toe." We danced as we worked, with all our might. By midnight, hunger would again grip the dancers, and a midnight dinner was spread for those who chose to eat. Many country boys learned to call for the dances. This writer did his part. There were good fiddlers, and they would play by turns. At my very earliest recollections, old man Fount Simmons was present at most of the dances and did most of the playing. I am not sure that he ever was surpassed as a fiddler.

Hardin County was never very productive for farming, and that was a long time before any of our society began selling the timber that grew all over the county. Our family's only source of living was the hogs that roamed the woods and got fat and the wild game that my father killed in the forest and brought home for food. There was no scarcity of wild game at that time. Many deer roamed the woods freely and hardly tried to conceal themselves because there was nothing much to be afraid of then. Thousands

24. A pre-Civil War log house.

of wild bear lived in the Big Thicket and got very fat every winter on the mast that grew on the oak trees in the forest. In the summer they would come out of the Thicket to the piney woods and prey on the hogs that ranged there. My father was one of the few men who lived in Hardin County, and during the summer months he

63

25. A pole barn.

and his neighbors spent much time hunting the wild bear that came out in the open woods to kill their hogs. In the winter when the bear were fat they made very fine meat, and my father used to go back in the Thicket to kill them and bring them home for food.

Pa killed hogs and cleaned them and put them on benches in the smokehouse; and then my mother would go in and cut the meat up in pieces and salt it and place it carefully in boxes and let it stay in there until it had taken the salt. Then she would take the meat and hang it on sticks in the smokehouse to dry. I think she did this because she wanted to, because I have heard her say that she could not trust Pa to do it right and she did not want the meat to spoil.

I do not know when my father got the spinning wheel and loom, but I know that it was very early in my parents' married life because they had no other means of getting clothes for their children, and there were six children when I was born. The only way to get clothes was for my mother to spin the thread; then with her superior knowledge of making cloth, she would sit down in front of that old loom and shuffle the shuttle from one side to the other until she had one great big piece of cloth in the loom to remove and cut into garments for the children to wear. And not just the children—she spun and wove her own clothes and clothes for my father. She never complained; she was always at work and she worked hard. I have heard that old spinning wheel going many nights until nine and ten o'clock.

Yard after yard she would weave, and maybe all seven of us would get a garment out of the cloth. I know when I was five years old my entire wardrobe consisted of two long-tail shirts. Ma wove the material. I suppose Pa got the long staple cotton some place, but my mother wove the cloth and she would cut out the garments and with the old sewing needle held in her dear old hands, she sewed the garments together so the children could wear them.

When she would get up in the mornings, she took pains to milk her own cows. She used to say that if two or three people were milking cows at the same time they would dry up, so she would not let anybody else milk. She would go to the cowpen and milk the cows and would let the calves suck, and afterwards she would turn the cows out to the range and leave the calves in the pen. She would then take the milk to the house and strain it and put it up to cream. That milk was not touched anymore until that night before she went to bed. Then it was carefully skimmed and the cream was put up into a bowl to go into the churning the next day. The skimmed milk she used for various purposes and sometimes we drank it. We always drank whole milk when we wanted it.

In the evening late, when the cows came up she would take her vessels and go to the cowpen again and would milk the four cows, and after she let the calves suck all they wanted, she would turn them out on the range that night and again she would take the milk into the house and strain it up to cream. Next morning she would put about two gallons of milk up to churn and put the cream in with it to clabber. Usually in warm weather the milk would clabber before night, and she would churn it and when the butter came she would take up the butter and wash it and would have a pound of good homemade butter for the family's consumption.

One thing she could not do and that was make shoes. When I was born there were three girls in the family. I do not think those girls ever wore homemade shoes. There were two or three little stores in the town of Hardin, and they carried things like very coarse cloth and coarse shoes. The girls' shoes were high topped, but they were typical brogans, and from the time I can first remember the girls were buying shoes from the store and they were surely proud of them. I know that each one of the girls knew what it took to make those shoes last, and they kept them soft while they lasted. They had tallow and they rubbed them almost daily, and it preserved them so they would hardly ever wear out.

But that did not count for the boys' shoes. Five boys came along right together. The oldest was seven years older than I was. I do not remember about his young days and whether he had shoes; but the next one, Brother Morg, was five years older than I, and from Morg on down we did not have any shoes. If it was too cold we stayed in the house; we were too small to do any work to amount to anything and we could stay by the fire. When summer came we did not need any shoes because the skin on the bottoms of our feet was so tough.

I remember I was in the old blacksmith shop Pa had close to the house, and one day he cut a piece of iron and threw it down. It was so hot it was almost white, but it was turning blue enough, so I stepped on it and stood on it until it burned and began to smoke. I was badly burned before I was able to feel the burn at all.

Well, we needed some shoes because we were getting large enough to do things and we could not get out without shoes, so my father told my mother that he was going to make us some shoes.

I remember the French people, the Guedrys, who came over from Louisiana and lived over on Batson Prairie, and I remember that they brought cattle with them and after a few years they had a large number. They killed and sold many beeves and accumulated many hides. Some enterprising Frenchman who had seen a tan yard somewhere decided he would put in one so he could sell the tanned leather. It was a fine business and my father knew about it.

He told my mother he would go over there to Batson Prairie to buy a hide to make us boys some shoes. He went on horseback and bought a big hide. He rolled it up tight and took that hide on the saddle in front of him, and I remember how proud I was when he brought the beef hide in because I was going to get some shoes. He began making shoes for the oldest and came on down to me (next to last); and after the various measurements of my foot, with a good sharp knife he cut the shoes out and put them on the last. He may not have been the finest shoemaker, but he could make them fast. I think within half a day I had some shoes. He fixed them so they would lace up and fixed holes in the vamps to put strings in so I could lace them. There was one thing—he always had a fine deer skin to cut strings from, and he cut my strings and I put the shoes on and I did not complain, but my feet, as hard as they were, could hardly bear those shoes. I tried to wear them but they were almost unbearable. Finally my mother said, "I will fix them for you; I will make you some yarn stockings tomorrow." She said that they would be so soft I could not feel the hard shoes. Well, that happened. She made the stockings and after that I could wear my shoes in comfort.

Then came the railroads and the sawmills, and one met many new faces wherever he went. The population of Hardin County

67

doubled between 1880 and 1890. The young people who once made merry in Old Hardin were scattered all up and down the railroad, and the newcomers brought new fashions in clothes, standards of life, and table manners. The principal changes I see are that the kernel is taken and the shell is left. They have thrashed the wheat and eaten the biscuits and left the chaff.

# GRANDMA HARRISON: A Day at Drew's Landing

BY ETHEL OSBORN HILL

*Ethel Osborn Hill (age eighty-seven) lives alone at the end of a two-rut, deep-sand road on her own forty acres, in a log house she built many years ago. The woods are deep around her Tyler County place, and the pine and sweet gum have grown high and close to the house. The 'coons and 'possums have pretty well accepted her as a kindred woods dweller, and they drop by periodically for left-overs. The squirrels feed from her hand, and the 'coons eat from plates nailed to the top of some nearby fence posts.*

*For a while a panther was coming by occasionally just to see if he could make her jump. The last time he came by it was the middle of the night, and Mrs. Hill waked up to hear him grunting and coughing as he wandered around the house. He scampered up a pine tree that grew close to the cabin and dropped off on the roof. After that it was poke around and sniff until he had satisfied his curiosity; then he sidled down the tree and was off again on his rambles. He killed a calf that night about two miles from Mrs. Hill's cabin and was forced to quit the country with a pack of hounds on his trail. He hasn't been back since, but if he does decide to return, there will be one person who will be glad to see him.*

*In spite of her eighty-seven years, Mrs. Hill is still a hopping little lady, as she has always been. During the 'twenties and 'thirties*

69

26. Ethel Osborn Hill.

*she was a journalist and syndicated columnist, writing for papers in Dallas, Houston, Beaumont, and other East Texas towns. Her story on Grandma Harrison (*BEAUMONT ENTERPRISE, *December 4, 1932) is the result of an interview with one of the most interesting of the Big Thicket settlers.—F.E.A.*

The Trinity River was rolling along like nobody's business on a bright fall day way back in 1860, but judging from the bustle and excitement along the river route, the business of the settlers was picking up in a big way. Laden with produce, they came on foot and by horseback and ox cart, forming a colorful assembly as they gathered at Drew's Landing on the Trinity River in the Big Thicket. Big doings were scheduled for the lively little river town, for it was "packet day," following

27.  Packet day—two river steamboats (Courtesy Clyde Gray's Heritage
Garden, Woodville).

long months of drought when "Ole Mistah Trinity" didn't have
enough water in it to float a raft, much less a packet boat.

Mrs. Lela Harrison came to the Big Thicket in the 1850's as a
tiny girl when her parents immigrated from Georgia. She has lived
all her life on the same land and recalls the glamorous days of the
river steamer traffic. On packet days she would load the big ox cart
with all manner of home-raised, home-prepared products and
drive to the wharf with the other settlers to buy and sell. Sometimes it was the *Belle of Texas,* sometimes the *Silver Cloud,* or
any one of the many packets which plied the Trinity and other
navigable East Texas streams at that time.

Grandma Harrison recalls the proud day when her load of products brought thirty-five dollars in cash, besides several items in
trade, which was unusual. That was the day when she had brought

28. The Hart house, built in the 1840's.

eleven gallons of bear oil, all rendered from one big, black bear which her husband had killed down at the wash hole.

Bear oil was always in demand by the boat captains and was always paid for in cash. It and other prime Big Thicket products—deer hides, bear, otter, and panther furs, tallow, wild honey, home-made palmetto hats, wooden casks of butter, tobacco and cotton—

would be carried from Drew's Landing on down to Liberty and then to Galveston or New Orleans. Bear oil and wild honey were usually put up in large gourds, often polished and beautifully decorated. A whittled wooden cork would serve as a stopper in the end of the long, slim neck, and a coating of beeswax made it air tight.

As the fame of the good hunting in the Big Thicket spread, more and more sportsmen sought it out. Hunting parties often came from as far away as Dallas, sometimes by horseback, sometimes by boat, and many of them stopped at the Harrison home. Because of Mrs. Harrison's hospitality—and she raised fifteen children during this time—she became known as "the mother of the hunters." "Many's the time," says Grandma Harrison, "that I've fed and bedded as many as twenty hunters in a day and a night. I've seen as many as thirty-five deer hanging in my yard at one time, and I'd always help them to cut up the carcass and jerk the meat, and help dress the skins, too."

During all those early years in the mid-nineteenth century, Grandma neighbored with the Alabama Indians, and "never were there better neighbors," declares Grandma. "In all the years we traded with them, I never knew one to steal, cheat, or break his word."

When Grandma Harrison's parents first came to the Big Thicket, the Alabamas were in a seemingly prosperous condition. There was fine hunting then; they raised good crops of corn, beans, squash, sweet potatoes, and tobacco. No one brought more or better goods to Drew's Landing on packet days than did the Indians. The women were adept at basket making, weaving, pottery, and bead work, and were quite skilled in cooking, especially meats and vegetables. Corn was always their staple food.

Sun-Kee, the chief who ruled the tribe when Mrs. Harrison was a little girl, lived to a great age. Grandma remembers him as a young, gorgeously dressed chief. Once, by invitation, she attended one of the Indians' elaborate ceremonies, the blessing of their first fruits and the giving of thanks to the god of sun and rain, Abba Mingo. She recalls the courtesy shown her by the chief.

Seated on a raised platform, he was dressed in full ceremonial robes and feathered headdress, a regal figure. Seeing Mrs. Harrison as she sat beneath a tree with her sleeping baby, he motioned her to approach. Taking the gorgeous blanket from around his shoulders, the chief spread it on the ground and, with a gesture of simple graciousness, took the sleeping baby from her arms and placed it thereon, saying kindly, "Now, Lela go see. Make dance, talk, eat. No be tired with papoose. Chief watch him good." So with the baby guarded by the chief, Lela saw the sights in the Indian village unhampered. This was in the 1870's, when the Alabamas still observed all of their tribal customs.

Grandma Harrison, far past her allotted three score and ten years, is still active and industrious and living on the land her forebears settled when they first came to the Big Thicket. Under the huge trees that shade her dooryard, she renders service to friends and neighbors as of old. It is still she who is called upon to dress the newborn, bake the wedding cake, and shroud the dead. She is living out the sunset of her life as busily as she lived her younger years.

# THE BATTLE AT BAD LUCK CREEK

BY DEAN TEVIS

*During the 1930's East Texas' spokesman in the field of history and legend was Dean Tevis, feature writer for the* BEAUMONT ENTER-PRISE. *Tevis regularly wandered the piney woods in search of the old legends and tales that were told about that country and its settlers. He knew just about everybody in the Big Thicket and recorded many stories that now, thirty years later, have been buried with the tellers.*

*Tevis's story of the Battle of Bad Luck Creek and Kaiser's Burn-out (*BEAUMONT ENTERPRISE, *October 25, 1931) is one version of a Civil War episode that left a distinct mark on the Big Thicket. The canebrake that was fired to flush out Warren Collins and the Big Thicket Jayhawkers never did grow back, and you can still see where Captain Kaiser and his men (in another version of the same story) left their fiery scar on the landscape.*

*There was another kind of mark left on the Thicket by the War, and this one also took a long time healing, if it ever has. That was left by the natural ill will that was felt between those men who went to the War and those who refused to go. It is always hard to say who shows the more courage in cases like theirs. The Jayhawk-ers were "union sympathizers" only in the sense that Sam Houston was; they weren't ready to see the United States broken in two. On*

75

29. Dean Tevis.

*the other hand, they weren't highly concerned with the political issues of any faction; they didn't have faction personalities. At one time, however, so another story goes, they all went down to Liberty to join up with a captain whom they particularly admired. But when they got there, military confusion and regimentation had taken over and they found that their leader had been sent to another area. Disgusted, they went back to the Thicket.*

*There's nothing certain about how long they had to hide out. They probably left their cabins and headed toward their Union Wells hideout every time they heard that the soldiers were getting ready to put the pressure on. When they ran low on salt or tobacco or other necessities, they robbed bee hives and took the honey to a pine hammock a few miles southeast of their camp to leave in exchange for whatever they needed. The little town at that location is still known as Honey Island.*

*Captain Charlie Bullock descended on the Jayhawkers sometime during the fall of 1864 and captured one band of them, including Warren Collins. Bullock marched them back to Woodville and jailed them in an old board-and-batten shack and put them*

30. A bee tree.

*under guard. The soldier failed to search Warren closely enough, however, and he was able to keep a small pearl-handled pen knife that he had hidden in his boot. After everything had settled down, the men began whittling away at the 1 x 12 siding where it joined the floor and soon had it to where it would swing out far enough for a man to squeeze through. Then Warren went up to the front and put on a show, dancing the buck and wing for the guards, while his comrades slipped out and headed back to the Thicket. When the guards saw that their prisoners were gone, they took off in all directions looking for them and Warren slipped out and hid under the jail. He rested there until everything had quieted down that night; then he crawled out and headed for home.*

*The last episode of the Jayhawker legend occurred in the spring of 1865 when Captain Bullock called for assistance from the Confederate fort in Galveston. Captain James Kaiser was sent with a troop of soldiers to Woodville, and Kaiser and Bullock proceeded to march to the Thicket and ring the Union Wells hideout with soldiers and finally with fire. Before the flames died out, three thousand acres had been burned and two Jayhawkers had been killed. The rest had escaped. The maneuver was so abortive that Captain Bullock quit the chase and the Jayhawkers finished that last year of the war in peace.*

*Tevis's version of this legend has a happy ending, with the Jayhawker leader and the Confederate captain going off on a hunt together after the War. One of the Jayhawker's many great-grandchildren told me that Warren Collins caught Charlie Bullock in Woodville after the War and gave his plow one good cleaning. You might call this the last battle of the Civil War in the Thicket. After that, the two warriors called a truce and were friends to the end of their days.—F.E.A.*

Pungent ashen-blue smoke from the remnants of a threatening woods fire floated across the hand-hewn picket fences of the Sutton clearing. An old yellow dog, lame in the "near hind leg," flopped with a thud, as though strength had suddenly fled him, to the bare sandy ground at the foot of worn pine stems. The nearest neighbor was four miles distant. Only a trail, pretty dim in places, led to the clearing. The thicket was tangled, its depth mysterious, rich in all the native trees and flowering shrubs with which East Texas woods, and especially the Big Thicket, have been lavished. Save for a scattered cut of some of the larger pines, made several years ago by a fast-moving logging crew, the Thicket was just as the first white man found it. The touch of autumn was upon it, and above it floated a blue-white bridge of Gulf-blown clouds, an arc of great slowly shifting stepping stones—above and in the surrounding thicket there was life, action, but the clearing itself, the only man-made thing within vision, presented a picture of dim bygones.

Aunt Cordelia Sutton, in a patterned calico which hung loosely about her and touched the ground, sat in a rawhide-bottomed chair. Few days would intervene before Aunt Cordelia would be seventy-five. She was two years old in 1856 when her father brought her from Georgia in an ox-drawn covered wagon from the seat of which her baby eyes watched the slow-changing scenery. Her little caravan was one of the company which plodded westward by devious ways over pioneer trails from east of the Sabine and beyond the Mississippi to a land of adventure—Texas. But the time-worn and smoke-blackened chair she sat in, and others occupied by members of the family, the Hickmans, was older even than Aunt Cordelia. Some of them were here when the white-topped wagons arrived. From some the back slats had long since dropped out and been lost—and that, likewise, was what nearly happened to the story of a sharp little incident in northern Hardin County history, a sort of footnote, if you please, of the Civil War.

That was the tale of the Battle of Bad Luck Creek, the story Aunt Cordelia—they called her "Aunt Deal"—was to tell one early afternoon on the gallery of the unpainted, picturesquely lonely back-country house in the depths of the Hardin County thicket.

The Battle of Bad Luck Creek is but one of the many forgotten incidents which the recounter of a history must, perforce, pass over, but which belong nevertheless in a book of the real romance of those days from '61 to '65. Your historian regards the game as it moves en masse from edge to edge of the board. This is the story of but one small, obscure move. It occurred within a stone's throw of this same spot one October morning in 1863. The clearing (or rather a short succession of them in the woods along the hidden flank of Bad Luck Creek) originally was made by the Collins family, whose descendants are scattered over Texas.

Time was, back in the '60's and before, when it bore some small importance on the map, but the Collins left and the clearing slipped slowly backwards into peaceful oblivion. Even Uncle Bud Brackin at Honey Island could give you only a fair general idea of where you'd find the trail in, for it's been a "smart few years" since he killed his last black bear up that way. County roads seemed to go everywhere but in that direction. Once the clearings lay on the Village Mills-Saratoga Highway. It was a highway—at least, of sorts. Previous to that it had been an Indian trail. The Alabamas knew it.

Signs on great beech trees, queer dimming marks made by strange hatchet blades, (beneath which that odd, silent sect, the "money hunters," have dug holes in the soft woods ground) point to its once having been traversed by the Spanish. And, if anyone cares to preserve historic keepsakes of East Texas, one or two of these old markings should be carefully removed and saved. Within a mile or two of where Aunt Deal smokes her pipe of evenings, there are several such relics. There are peculiar beliefs that beneath each of the carvings lies gold—treasure of some sort—but one is a little doubtful that the traveling Spanish, largely afoot, could carry enough gold to favor the vicinity of each tree they marked—if the Spanish did mark them. Perhaps the markings carried definite messages for friends who were to follow. Chief Charley, the Indian chief with an English name, is one of the few who can recount a story of how the marks came to be on the trees. He had it from his grandmother.

Today the settlers refer to the old highway near the clearing as the "Throwed Away Road." If you follow its fading tracks across a little-used ford in Cypress Creek near the crumbling bones of a once sturdy wagon bridge it will take you past the site of the Holland home, and near one of the spots where the Alabamas had their village. It runs through an unblemished country where deer are almost as numerous as they were half a century ago. Cloud-high virgin longleaf, placid magnolia, and Yuletime holly, little pin oaks, and sweet gum; ironwood for the bow and ash for the arrow; or yet hickory for your stock or the rungs of your pioneer's chair, set off by silver-plated elm, by redbud—coquette of the woods—and by the April bride, East Texas' fast-disappearing dogwood. Here happily you seldom see the telltale mark of a chopped limb. They spread their arms and bloom in intermittent shade in the glory that was once all of the Mexican impressario's grant. Save for a crew of pipeliners, who parted the Thicket's stubborn locks in the middle, few trespass the wilderness—for wilderness it surely is, and no place for a low-hung car.

The Sutton clearing and the site of the battle lie near the northwestern corner of the county, seven or eight miles from the border of Polk, and some few miles south of Tyler. Bad Luck Creek itself is a happy struggling little stream, dry as a bone when rains are few but a torrential personality in a season of storms. It makes a union with Cypress Creek, a member of the upper house of Hardin's creeks, at a point where eerie cypress knees reach up with their round brown knobs to touch Spanish moss which falls as though by certain design of the wood artist, from the boughs of its mother, the oak. It is one of the most beautiful and fecund patches left anywhere in east Texas, a place where one may say— "This is as it once was."

While man and time have been kind to the forest, neither have the seventy intervening years changed the Collins clearing one jot, save for the buildings. The older homes have gone, but the Sutton place, occupied by Aunt Deal, her nephew, Dick Jordans, and the Hickmans, is a sturdy carbon copy, they say, of the others. When you open the creaking picket gate, where the lolling dog looks up but doesn't summon the effort to growl, the leaves of

31. Warren Collins (Courtesy Cecil Overstreet).

time have flipped back for you. Even the briefest look about you affords the complete curtain, the backdrop, if you will, of your story.

The players stand in a row as if for a curtain call on the bank of the Bad Luck—the Collins men, big, raw-boned, handy with a trigger, and handy with an axe. There is Old Man Lilly, evidently older than the others, a harmless, pleasant old fellow, who wasn't interested in the doings of the Collinses or their friends, and much less the warfare in which they were engaged, but who got caught between the millwheels and fell with a severed gallus and a bullet through his heart. Then there was Ed Riley, who lived strangely enough to fight Indians in the west, and a Captain Mitchell, a leader of the militant minority in the little argument arising over —well, call it sectionalism.

Towering over all save Warren Collins is the memorable figure of Captain Charles Bullock of Woodville. Together they made a strange pair, who in the end saw that differences were futile and shook hands. Back of the Collinses stand their boys in nondescript homespuns and wool hats tattered from briars. Behind the mounted figure of Bullock are his men, in Confederate gray, each on horse and each bearing a breech-loader across the pommel. They all step backwards, the Collins followers with their rifles handily in the crooks of their supple arms, for the two central figures to take their bows.

Then come the facts in the story, trooping along with a quick-step. Under the spell of the almost lost clearing (which it wouldn't be wise to try to find without a clever guide) and the magic of an aged woman, the drama, with its touch of comedy, is built up in strong colors.

When Texas, against the hard-fought effort of Sam Houston, joined the secession movement and left the Union, there were those who sympathized with old San Jacinto. Here and there bands formed to oppose conscription because they favored the other side, or because, while their hearts were really with Texas, they wouldn't bear arms against either side. One of these was the Collins band—known far and wide over several counties of East Texas as Union sympathizers. Their headquarters were the clearings of the two Collins homes. They ranged between there and a spot on the Polk County line now known as Kaiser's Burnout, or the Union Wells.

Union Wells is the older title, born of the fact that the northern adherents (really at heart pure southerners) dug three wells in the woods, camouflaged them with tree branches and leaves, and used them for a water supply when the creeks ran dry. You can find these wells today.

83

Often the band, afoot but well armed, was hard pressed for sufficient food. At least for bread and salt. The number is given variously at from fifteen to twenty. Frequently they came to the Collins cabins. One of these was occupied by Warren Collins. The other was the home of his brother Stace, and in one or the other lived Newt, a third brother.

The skirmish with the Union men, dignified later with the name "battle," has become legend. If the details of its story were ever recorded upon a printed page the record has not come to light. So the beads of fact, strung upon their yellowing string, must of necessity be drawn from the tales told by the oldest of the woods folk of today. One of the best versions is that of Aunt Cordelia, as she has told it many a time.

At the time of the Bad Luck battle she didn't live in the clearing but rather in the settlement in Hardin near what is now Hooks' Switch. Yet her story can be relied upon. The Collins of Dallas will tell you this. She, as well as others who contributed these facts, had them from the lips of the participants, all of whom have gone. F. B. Prince, who knew Grandpa Warren Collins, as everyone came to know him, helps fill in what missing patches there are in the quilt. In fact, Prince is remarkable among other things, for his knowledge of Hardin County, as well as general Texas history.

The action of the tale begins with the formation, by Captain Bullock of Woodville, of the Bullock Cavalry. This was a body of soldiery, home guards, or Confederate militia, formed under a commission of the Confederate government and the state, to take care of an often troublesome and constantly fermenting situation at home. The nearest federal troops were across the Sabine. One of the jobs cut out for Bullock was to capture any banded northern sympathizers. His territory lay from Woodville clear to the Salines of the coast. So there came to his attention the case of the little band in Hardin County. It is fairly well established, and quite logical to assume, that Bullock and Bullock's men were well acquainted with the Collins and their men. But the conscription board wanted them and he had to try to rout them out. The band, peaceable enough if left alone, maintained a camp near the Union

32. Captain Charles Bullock (Courtesy Mrs. J. P. Tolar).

Wells on the Polk County border. Up in that country was a settler by the name of Kaiser, or Kiser, an old German they say, for whom the country was named. The territory was a dense thicket of woods and canebrake—an ideal place for a hasty hideout.

Bullock evidently saw it was hopeless to try to invade the place. The Union men had their sentries out, sharp-eyed fellows, and they were pretty secure from capture. His own men were not well acquainted with the country. But the Collins boys and their friends certainly were. So the soldiers were at a distinct and unpleasant disadvantage.

Then came the browning fall of 1863, accompanied by a long dry spell and followed by a brisk norther—then only torches were needed to send the band out and southward. Fire was the one thing they couldn't withstand; so the militia leader ordered that fire be set to the canebrakes and the woods. The men set the blaze in a sort of horseshoe shape, knowing that the Union band was in the center of the furnace they were creating. Near the hideout was a spot called "Painter's Den," for the reason that many woods panthers, or wildcats, took up their habitat there. That name, as well as the "Burnout," and Union Wells, will stick as long as Texas. Within brief minutes, fanned by the norther and fed by the dry undergrowth, the fire swept into a fury. But the Woodville leader's men queerly left the horseshoe open from the south. The only thing they really accomplished was to rout the men and burn the country. They couldn't hope to capture them when they had left this loophole. For a distance of three miles and more, as they will show you today, and over a swath of a half-mile in breadth, the flames cleaned the country out. The trees never came back and the country became a prairie strangely in the midst of the Thicket. For more than a century it has been referred to as "The Burnout" or "Kaiser's Burnout."

The fire left the Union sympathizers with one less refuge than before. So they trekked southward and east in the direction of the cabins in the Collins clearings—home.

And now there treads up the boards to the footlights one Lilly— they called him Old Man Lilly. His was the oddest and most unfortunate case of the lot. He was the single victim of the battle and his bones lie in an unmarked but not forgotten grave in the Sutton burial ground near the cabin. Lilly, like the others, was a woods settler. His home, another mud-chinked log cabin about which lay a typical cabin atmosphere, was across the line in Polk County. Distances were great through the woods if measured by miles, but they were shortened by the fact that neighbors were few. An unkind, unfair fate led him into a position between the opposing forces.

Some days prior to the brief affair on Bad Luck Lilly had traded,

86

33. Kaiser's Burnout.

in pioneer fashion, with some of the Collins for a wagon. And while the battle was brewing in the woods kettle, he was traveling from Polk County southward to the Collins clearing driving a yoke of oxen. They, too, were valuable in those days. He hoped that on the return journey he'd have the oxen hitched to the wagon.

34. Bad Luck Creek.

You can easily see him traveling along, plodding the oxen through thickets, singing (perhaps "Come to the Bower"), as he thought of the folks in the Polk County cabin. On the way south luck favored him, so the story goes, with a successful shot at a red deer. So he stayed the night in the woods to dress it. Save for that venison he would have had his wagon and been on his way home— but then the story of Bad Luck wouldn't have been worth writing.

It was early on the morning of a sunny day when he came in sight of the Stace Collins clearing. He hailed the family, entered the house, and was having breakfast—a breakfast of cornpone and squirrel legs—and enjoying it, when the sound of shots was heard. Lilly, as Aunt Deal tells it, whipped out of the door, his jacket tails flying, just at the right moment to come between Captain Bullock's muzzle-loaders, and the little band which the Confederate militia thought they had trapped.

He ran, but was shot down. The bullet which slew him cut his galluses.

One of the militiamen remarked to his fellow troopers nearby, "When you find a man with his galluses busted, he's mine. I shot him!"

Aunt Cordelia is the only person who knows who shot Lilly. She might tell you his name if you'd catch her just right, sort of such a time as when the blue smoke from a timber fire is graying the clearing. She lives, while she putters about her chores, in the days that used to be.

It seems, according to best accounts of the affair, whose story-threads will never all be gathered together, that the militia had split into two parties following their firing of the woods. One rode to the Stace Collins home and the other to the home of Warren Collins. Like Stace's cabin and narrow clearing which grew the corn for the pone, Warren's home was situated on, or quite near, the bank of Bad Luck. At the moment with which this particular part of the story deals the creek, according to some versions, had no name. But the next day they began calling it "Bad Luck."

The militia contingent assigned to the Warren Collins clearing was given a special order. Warren was looked upon as the most

89

dangerous man of the opposing company, possessing a rare marksmanship and a rare courage. So the spoken order was to "get Warren first."

Bullock rode up and asked the woman if Warren was in the house. His wife, alone with several children, told him her husband was not there. The house was searched and then the men drew off. A short time later Warren did come up, carrying with him the carcass of a deer. His wife begged him to leave, but he said he had come for breakfast and nothing could rob him of it. Meals for the boys who refused to wear the grey were often few and far between. When he did go his wife ran the long distance through the woods to warn the others that the Bullock forces were in the neighborhood. A tense stillness settled over the forests. There was sharp expectancy. One didn't know just what was going to happen, nor who would fall before whose guns!

In the meantime action was about to open at the Stace Collins cabin, occupying about the same situation in the clearing as the Sutton house does today. The other wing of the Bullock cavalry had come up, failed to find their men, warned the women not to make their presence known, and withdrawn to a nearby but hidden position in the deep woods to watch and wait. Then, fearlessly, the Union men soon came to the cabin for breakfast. They were the black markers, surrounded, checkmated, by the red—the forces, one greatly outnumbering the other, met in the yard. Lilly fled between them and was the only one to die. With one exception the entire band escaped. Bullock's sharpshooters had the draw on Stace Collins and he went down on the clearing ground with a shattered hip bone.

He was not taken prisoner, but was cared for in a cabin which always afterwards was known as "the hospital place." A fever rose rapidly. Stace was dangerous ill. No physicians. But the settlers, often wiser than we knew, allowed cold water to drip constantly on the wound—and Stacy got well and lived to be an old, old man.

There is no report that any of the militiamen were hit by the woodsmen's hand-molded bullets. When the men saw they were outnumbered and neatly trapped they took to the woods. Bullock, as a soldier, sometimes steps out sharply, but in the case of the Bad Luck battle your strategists can't give him much. A little more planning and there would have been a far different tale to be told.

After that, for a while at least, the Union men were cautious. A story has it that Grandma Riley, a staunch figure of the early Hardin wilderness, who lived to travel with her grandson into West Texas long after the Civil War, had a verbal encounter with Captain Bullock on the streets of Sour Lake—in which the Woodville man came off second best.

With the end of the war the Collins and their followers returned to their homes, and a quiet which hasn't been broken to this day reigned again in that part of Big Thicket. The day they clear the depths of the Thicket will be the day when the last vestige of old times will have passed.

From former Senator V. A. Collins of Dallas comes an angle of the Bad Luck story which pleasantly refutes the origin given above for the creek's name. According to Senator Collins his father, the memorable Warren Collins, named it before the Civil War. He was a hunter who always found game. The woods were full of it—deer, bear, turkeys. But hunt as diligently as he might he couldn't bag a squirrel, it appears, near the little creek running past his cabin. So one day he remarked that he was going to name it "Bad Luck."

The name fits well in either case, and one certain fact is that as long as the creek rolls down the Hardin divide toward Cypress Creek and Village, the mother creek, and on to the Neches, it won't ever be changed.

Half a decade passes from the epoch of the Bad Luck battle and we find two men in their thirties smoking pipes on a blackened cabin gallery. Turn the kaleidoscope ever so little and the same pair appears on narrow steps of a little wooden courthouse at Woodville. Perhaps one has his arm across the other's shoulders.

Another little turn and the colored pebbles show them walking the woods, each with a long rifle. They are most amiable this time, though their guns are in the crooks of their arms. They're

91

old cronies, if you please—this same Warren Collins and Captain Charles Bullock of Woodville.

They've made up their differences—The cloud bridge breaks into a mottled group of tumbling shapes, forms again, and the sun falls a little farther into the west. Presently the pines hide it. Shadows are long. Warren and the captain go deeper and deeper into the magnolia-scented woods, and night falls.

# BUCKSHOT AND BLUE WHISTLER
## An Interview with Frank Herrington

BY FRANCES PITTS NORVELL

*Hampton Jackson Herrington didn't believe in slaveholding; his father did. So after a long-running argument, Hamp left home. He married Rachel Overstreet and started farming near Montgomery, Alabama. They had five children before she died in 1844. As was frequently the case in those days, the family was ready to look out after each other, and Rachel's sister came to live with Hamp and look after the house and the children. As Enoch Bentley Herrington tells it:*

After Rachel's death, my grandmother, Elizabeth, and her mother were staying at Grandfather's house, taking care of the two children then living, Lum and John. My grandmother said the only courtship she and Grandpa ever had was one day at noon she was on the front porch and had just finished washing the faces of Lum and John and was putting clean dresses on them when Grandpa came up on steps at the end of the porch, took a gourd of water in his hand, took a long drink while he was kicking off his plow shoes, and said, "Well, Becky, it looks like you are going to have to stay here and attend to the children so I'm going to town Saturday and if you are willing I'll get the license and bring the preacher and we'll be married."

Grandma said she replied, "All right, Hamp."

*Hamp was looking for greener pastures and deeper woods by 1853, and his family and a family of Overstreets and of Masons*

35. Frances Pitts Norvell at eighteen years.

36. B. F. (Frank) Herrington (Courtesy Miss Ruby Herrington).

*started out for Texas in two-wheeled carts. They were three
months getting from Alabama to the Big Thicket. Hamp built a
big square log house for his family and settled down and began to
thrive. He prospered, helped organize Hardin County in 1858,
and was the county's first magistrate, holding his first court under
a dogwood tree in Old Hardin. Hampton Herrington had seven
sons, one of whom was Frank Herrington, who tells the following
story of hunting in the Big Thicket.*

*Mrs. Frances Pitts Norvell, who took down the Frank Herring-
ton story, is kin to Frank, in a distant sort of way. But then just
about everybody in the Thicket is kin to everybody else.*

*Enoch Pitts, Mrs. Norvell's uncle, came to the Thicket before
the Civil War, and when the War came along he signed up with
a lot of other Hardin County boys. He made it through the War,
but he didn't make it back to his wife Fannie and his children.
Enoch and a friend were spending the night in a hotel in Rich-
mond, Virginia, on their way home. When the time came to go to
bed, instead of turning off the gas-mantle lamps, they blew them
out and settled down for a last long sleep.*

*Jacob, Enoch's brother, was foot-loose after his discharge from
the Confederate Army; so he headed for the Village Creek home
of his brother's widow. Here was another case where they decided
to stay with the family. Jacob married Fannie, and Frances Pitts
Norvell was one of their children. She grew up in the Thicket,
knows it well, and loves it, and collected some interesting tales
when she was writing her book.—F.E.A.*

I will tell you how people hunted when I was a
small boy. They would go out in the woods and
find deer in herds of from three to fifteen. While the deer were
feeding, the hunter would walk very slowly until he was a right
distance to make a kill; he would pick out the one he wanted, bang
went the gun, down fell the deer, dead. The hunter made no wild

95

shots for he knew he had only one chance: the gun he used was a cap and ball.

The hunter reloaded his gun by measuring the powder first. He poured this into an old long rifle, and a piece of strong cloth was then laid over the end of the gun. The hunter, taking one bullet and pressing it down on the cloth until it was all even, took his knife and cut off the cloth smooth all around. The wooden stick, called a ramrod, was used to force the bullet down tight on the powder. The cap was placed on the tube, and the hunter was ready for the hunt.

Still hunting was the only way people hunted in those early days. Yes, we had dogs, but we did not let them run anything but vermin. If a dog chased a deer, his owner caught him, tied a small rope around his neck, and threw one end of the rope over the limb of a tree. He would hang the dog just high enough so his hind feet touched the ground. He then gave the dog about forty hard lashes with a switch about three feet long. That dog would not chase any more deer.

I don't remember the first time that I saw a breech-loading shotgun. I was probably about twelve years old. My brother bought a twelve-gauge, single-barrel shotgun. I was anxious to shoot it. One day about an hour before sundown, I was allowed to use the gun. I went across the branch of the creek, about one hundred yards from our old home, then on another three hundred yards. All at once up jumped a big buck. I cracked down on him, and he fell almost in his tracks. I stood still; another small deer jumped up about twenty-five yards from me. I shot him dead. Two more deer came galloping by me, fifty or sixty feet from me; I shot at one of them. He fell, then got up again. I fired another shot that laid him sprawling on the ground. There were three deer, dead, inside of a fifty-foot circle. The distance from where the deer lay to my home was less than a quarter of a mile. Boy, oh boy! You should have heard me shouting. My brother had heard the shots and when I began hollering, they all came running to me. They were all glad to see my kill and glad that I had not shot myself. This was my first hunting experience.

37. Uncle Bud Brackin claimed 305 Big Thicket bears to his credit (Courtesy Osborne Wiggins).

Fifty years ago there were all kinds of wild game in the Big Thicket. Deer, turkey, black bear, wild cat, wolves, panthers, 'possum, 'coon, pole cat, squirrels, rabbits, and other varmints. Now game is not so plentiful, but there are still many wild animals. One day, when I was walking on a lonely road, on the edge of the Big Thicket—I was grown then—I heard some dogs barking. As I was familiar with the voices of the dogs, I knew they belonged to Bud Brackin and Jake Lloyd. These were bear dogs. People at this time trained their dogs to run different animals and varmints. I stopped by the side of the road and looked through the woods to see what was coming my way. The sage grass was so

38. Present-day hunters stand by a pine-knot fire and listen to the hounds.

tall I could not see anything at first. It was not long, however, till I saw something big and black coming toward me. There I was with no gun, so I stayed by the tree. On came the big black bear, hot and foaming at the mouth. There was a small pond of water near the tree. When the bear saw the water, he just plunged right into it. I decided to let him see me, so I just raised my hat and said, "Good morning." The bear raised up on his hind feet, his hair all turned up. He opened his mouth and made a funny noise. The dogs were now so close to him that he decided to leave. Right through the woods went the bear, dogs, and all. Then came Mr. Brackin and Jake Lloyd. As Jake passed me, he asked me if I had seen his dogs.

I said, "Yes, I saw two dogs and a bear going toward the Parker Place."

Brackin and Lloyd crept in where the dogs and bear were and killed the monster. The bear was extra large. They blew their horn, and I went to them and helped them put the bear on one of their horses. After we had discussed his weight, we decided he would weigh four hundred pounds or more. Mr. Lloyd and Mr. Brackin were winter bear hunters; there were no game laws then. Most every winter they would kill about forty bears.

In Hardin County there used to be many panthers. I have never seen but two panthers in these woods, though. They seemed to be the first of the wild animals to leave the Big Thicket, I have heard my mother and father say. My folks came to Hardin County in 1849 and settled the old Herrington Place. The first year they lived there, my father and his neighbors killed thirteen panthers, not over three quarters of a mile from their home. One night, a panther caught a pig in the chimney corner. My father turned his varmint dogs loose. He and the dogs killed the panther.

Once, I lived in Saratoga, Texas. I was there when the great oil boom came in 1901. Before the oil boom, I farmed and raised hogs in the Big Thicket. It was easy to raise hogs there, for acorns and roots were plentiful enough to furnish a goodly portion of their food. I kept some well-trained dogs, and one special dog named Sam. He would go right into the thickest jungle and round up a bunch of hogs and do a good job. One morning I was riding out into the woods at the head of Black Creek; this was a most desolate country, and Mr. Ben Hooks had killed many black bear near here. My dog Sam was going along in front of me. All at once he looked back at me. I told him to go ahead, and he did. In less than five minutes, I heard him bark; thinking it was a sow with young pigs, I lighted off my pony and went creeping into the woods. The palmetto and ty-vine were so thick I could not see the ground. Just as I got near the spot where Sam was baying, I discovered a huge red-oak tree that had blown down. I eased along until I got onto the roots of this tree. I walked slowly until I came to some limbs above the heavy underbrush. Everything was quiet but Sam. He was barking for life. I ventured a little farther out on two of these limbs, one foot on one limb, and the other foot on the other limb. I was now a long distance from the ground, say about eight feet. All at once, I heard a sniff and up rose a big old yellow-mouthed bear. I guess he had scented me; he turned around and came waddling toward me. On he came and passed under my feet. You can say what you please, but he looked as big as a Ford car. There I was again without a gun. I did not even have a pocket-knife. The bear went on fourteen or fifteen feet and turned his big face toward me. I held my breath for a minute. Then he decided to leave. He went through the palmetto and ty-vine. Sam followed and stopped him. I went back to my horse and gave my horn a toot. Sam quit the bear and came back to me. We decided to hunt no more hogs that day.

Because I had such a fine dog, my neighbors were always asking me to help them round up their hogs and other stock. This I was glad to do. One day Uncle Henry Teal asked me to go to a place called Ty-Vine Thicket. We got a daylight start the next day, going on horse back four or five miles; then we left our horses and went on foot. Sam was anxious to go, but I had not told him to go ahead. We had not gone far when I saw Sam's nose in the air as though he was scenting. In five or eight minutes I told him to go ahead. We heard him barking in a place so thick with trees and underbrush one could scarcely crawl through it. We got down on our hands and knees and started crawling toward the dog. Mr. Teal was a few feet ahead of me. All at once, he stopped and motioned me to look beyond him. I pushed the underbrush aside in order to see. There sat a big old bear as black as the ace of spades. He was rolling his eyes from side to side and watching the dog at the same time. Neither of us had a gun. We had left them tied to our saddles with our horns. We were within fifteen feet of the bear. After a moment, we left him with the situation. We crawled backward to a place where we could stand up. When we reached our horses, we decided to let the bear go so I blew my horn for Sam. When he came out we continued our hog hunt.

There is a place in the Big Thicket called the Union Wells, so called because the men who did not go to the War between the States hid in these dense woods. Men who hunt in the Thicket go

39. A Saratoga bear hunt in 1910 (Courtesy Clyde Gray's Heritage Garden, Woodville).

to this place so they will have plenty of water. One day a friend of mine, Fount Simmons, who lives at Votaw, said to me, "Frank, suppose you and I make up a big deer hunt and go to Union. Wells."

I said, "That will be fine, Fount."

We got word to the men and started the next day. There were thirteen of us in the crowd, all on horse back. Some of the men carried cap and ball guns, some Winchesters, and some shotguns. Fount was our leader; he knew all the woods around there. We carried with us seven of the best trained hounds that were ever in Hardin County. These dogs were all about the same size and color. They were white and blue speckled. The name of the start dog was Blue. I still remember the names of the men on the hunt: Dan Overstreet, Dan McNeely and his son, George Sims, Sheer-

101

wood Holland, H. D. Herrington, my brother, and others. We went on a wagon road as far as Dan Overstreet's, and then we followed a trail about nine miles. From there we traveled Indian style, one behind the other, until we got to Union Wells.

Fount was in the lead; he looked back at me and said, "Frank, how about me letting old Blue take a chase around; he might run a deer by us."

I said, "All right."

Fount was carrying a ten-gauge shotgun; I also had a ten-gauge. In his gun were buckshots, and in mine were larger shots called blue whistlers. Blue galloped out in the woods at Fount's command. Two hundred yards from us he jumped a deer; here they came running, kinder girting around us. We stopped when the deer got in about fifty yards of us. I raised my gun and cracked down; the buck fell.

I said, "You see I can flirt them, Fount."

He looked straight at me and said, "Shake me, I killed him."

Green was the next man to me and he said, "No fooling, boys, you both shot at the same time."

Fount said, "All right, boys, I shot the deer. A dead shot, I know."

I spoke up, "Well, I think I broke his neck; I tried to do that."

We all dismounted from our horses and went to look at the deer. There he lay, a big old ten-pointer. On examination, it was found that we were both right: Fount had shot the deer behind the shoulder, and I shot him in the neck—buckshot and blue whistler. We put the deer on the horse and went on to our camping ground, from where we continued our hunt for several days.

Just before we got to camp, up jumped a big doe. My brother was the hindmost one in the trail so he got this shot and down the deer fell. We carried this one by hand as it was only a short distance to our camping place. We then took out the entrails and cut off the head.

Next we arranged for our camping. We tied our horses and fed them. Our horses were tied almost in a half circle to small trees on the south side of our camp. We dressed both deer, cut them in

40. Killraine—dog handler, storyteller, cook, actor—whose name comes up every time old-time hunting stories are told (Courtesy J. A. McKim).

small strips, and put the meat on a frame we had built in order to dry our venison. We had to keep a fire going all night; and a little after dark, all decided to go kill some more deer. There were thirteen of us men in the crowd and only six headlights; so I proposed to stay at camp and let them go, two and two, all on foot. I was to stay at camp and blow my horn so as to keep the camp located for them. Off they went into the glades.

I heard two guns. I blew my horn. A slow rain drizzle had set in. I blew my horn and got an answer. In a few minutes I heard one gun and answered it again. By this time it was totally cloudy. They had all got out of hearing of my horn; I blew and blew my horn but got no answer. I waited a while, blew my horn; then I heard a scream some distance from me. I blew my horn and the scream came closer; I decided it was a panther. I had no light, nothing but some red coals under the meat that was cooking. On came the screamer. Out to one side of me about fifty or sixty yards was a hole of water. This monster came to the water and I heard him lapping some. Then our horses that were tied to the small trees began snorting and rearing against the ropes, but didn't break loose. I never did get to see the panther.

The hunters were all lost in the woods and didn't get in until next day. They went with me down to the hole of water and there were his tracks, but Fount's dog would not run him. This panther went on to the place where my brother butchered the big doe. The panther had eaten all the head and entrails that we had left there.

Long years ago, in the 1880's, I had a boy friend, a cousin of mine, whose name was Miles P. Jordan. His father's name was Thomas Jordan. Thomas lived on a farm in the Big Thicket, located four miles southeast of Saratoga, Texas. Thomas was a good farmer and a great bear hunter. He would kill from ten to twenty bears each winter. He would dry the meat and render up the bear oil, which provided meat and oil all the year round.

Thomas' farm was located only a short distance from a small bayou called Little Pine Island Bayou. He still hunted with his old muzzle-loading shotgun, an eight gauge. He called these shots lead slugs. These slugs were about the size of a marble. His gun was a double barrel, and when he got one of these slugs in each barrel and plenty of powder behind it, he could count on a sure kill. His son Miles and I didn't enjoy bear hunting so very much, so we each bought a breech-loading gun. Miles bought a forty-four gauge Winchester and I bought a ten-gauge double-barrel shotgun. We hunted ducks, turkeys, and deer. We always walked while hunting, calling it still hunting.

Miles and I went out one morning, just across the little bayou. We turned our course down the bayou some distance, approximately three quarters of a mile, feeling sure that a big deer would hop up soon. We were on a small branch called Wild Cat Branch which was so crooked you could hardly tell which way was downstream. I told Miles to take one side and I would take the other so when we got a deer going, if it ran toward him, I would give a whistle and vice versa. We had separated about 150 yards, and I saw a big tree that was uprooted. The palmetto and small brush were thick but anyone could see quite a distance by getting on a log. I got on a log and walked slowly toward its top. I had gone on this log about half way to the top and could see Miles. I stomped my foot down the log to make a noise to see what would happen, and up jumped a big old buck just a short distance from me. I could have killed him dead on the spot, but I saw he was headed toward Miles. I was more than anxious to see Miles shoot him with his new Winchester, so I gave a loud whistle. On the deer went, just missing Miles about forty yards. I saw Miles raise his gun and down came the deer.

We used to hunt with an old one-load rifle, a muzzle loader. We had the habit of always buckling on our big hunting knives; when we shot anything, we pulled out our knives to finish him up. Miles set his Winchester up by a tree, pulled out his knife and made for the deer. Just as he was within a few feet of the deer, it got up and started wobbling off through the thick palmetto. Miles undertook to outrun the deer, so round and round they went, until finally, they came to a little crooked branch. The deer would jump the branch then Miles would jump it. Finally Miles caught the deer by the tail. It just squatted down and by that time I was on the spot. I was laughing fit to kill at Miles.

"Why in the devil don't you help me?" he asked.

"Turn him loose and I'll get him."

Miles was afraid to turn him loose. He thought maybe I would miss him. At last he let the deer go. When he got a good start I shot and broke his neck. Miles kept looking at me and asked what had tickled me so. I told him that I was laughing at him for setting his gun down by the tree.

He thought a moment, then said, "Well, I did have sixteen more loads in that gun. Why didn't I think of that and use them instead of trying to use the knife?"

We went back home and that ended our hunt for the day.

I could tell a lot more stories about this country in which I was born seventy-five years ago. I thank the Lord for those happy years.

# CAMP BIG THICKET: Life in the Piney Woods, 1887

BY JOHN A. CAPLEN

*We don't know much about John Caplen—who he was, where he had come from, or where he was going—but the story he wrote for the* SUNNY SOUTH *(published in Atlanta, Georgia, in 1887) includes details of Big Thicket life that make it interesting on-the-spot reporting. Wherever he had come from, he hadn't been traveling a main road. And wherever he was going he passed through the old Buck Hooks farm near Thicket and through Batson Prairie. Buck was living on Batson Prairie on the southwestern edge of the Thicket in 1887, although he left the same year and went back to his farm in the heart of the Thicket. Buck built a board-and-batten salt-box house there in the 1890's, and his son Ben (called "Little" Ben to distinguish him from Uncle Ben) built a fine dog-trot house next to him around 1900. Little Ben's house is still there, sagging a bit, and the old split shingle roof is green with moss and resurrection fern, but the place is still as pretty a picture of old-time East Texas architecture as you can find nowadays.— F.E.A.*

I have been in the heart of the "Big Thicket" in Polk and Hardin counties, Texas, for ten days. Nothing can be seen except the tangled underbrush and tall trees.

107

41. Little Ben Hooks' house, near Thicket.

In a ride of 150 miles through these two counties, there is one continuous dense growth of tall pines—oaks, magnolias, and numerous other forest trees. As far as the eye can see, it is the same; the tangled undergrowth and fallen trees block and interpose an almost impassable barrier in the way of any kind of vehicle. In

42. A cypress horse trough.

many places we have to get down on our hands and knees to
crawl through the thick, close-knitted growth of baygall bushes
and canebrakes. Not a human being can be seen for miles. A dim
trail through the thicket is all we have to guide our way; the eyes
of our guide are constantly scanning the ground so as to follow
the trail. A feeling of awe and desolation comes over me as I look
up and around at the big pine trees, white oaks, and magnolias
that we pass in pushing our way through the canebrakes. Not a
voice is heard except our own; and when we are passing a grove

of pines, the moaning of the wind makes us feel as if the Judgment Day was about to come.

After riding twenty miles, following our guide, we came to a clearing in the woods. It was with pleasure that we alighted from our tired horses. The dogs commenced to bark, and presently there emerged from the house our very kind and hospitable friend, Buck Hooks. Buck is a true Texan, and has a nice home on the edge of the prairie. He is the most expert woodsman in this part of the country and knows every spot in the Big Thicket. He can come in and go out at any time, night or day; I believe he knows every tree. His cattle feed on the rich cane abounding everywhere in the Thicket; they become very wild in there, and it requires a trained and expert woodsman to handle them or drive them to the prairie. It often happens that the only way the cattle can be gotten out of the Thicket is to shoot them, take the hide, and leave the carcass to the wolves and bears to have a treat on. My friend Buck has a farm in the heart of the Thicket. A real kind, old-fashioned fellow, by the name of W. F. Smith, lives there with his family, and they all appear to be contented and happy (although he has to ride twelve miles and back through a dim trail in the thicket for a sack of meal, every week).

The people who live in the pine woods of Eastern Texas are very primitive in their habits. As this was the first part of Texas that was settled by the early pioneers, their descendants form the principal part of the population. Traveling through the deep piney woods of this part of Texas, you often find grown men and women that have never seen any prairie country, mountain or valley, railroad or steamboat. They grow to manhood and womanhood in the heart of the thicket pine woods, and are contented and happy in their log cabins. Oh, contentment, what a blessing! Their diet would by no means please the stomach of an epicure. Cornbread, bacon, and potatoes, with an occasional treat of venison, gives them perfect satisfaction. Nearly all the children born and reared in the pine woods have light hair; it is a rare sight to see a dark-haired family.

43. A dog trot in the Pelt house, near Saratoga.

Very few of the descendants of the old settlers own any land.
For the last forty years they have been in the habit of settling upon
any land fit for cultivation. After finding a good, rich land (hammock) the piney woods settler will commence felling and cutting
the trees and underbrush away from where he will have a log

rolling. His wife makes preparations for a big dinner and all his neighbors, for miles around, come and pile up the logs that have been cut down, then put the brush in piles and set them on fire. In a few days his field is all cleared and ready for the plow. After working someone else's land for two or three years, he sells the improvements and his squatter's claim to one of his neighbors, and then hunts up another place or piece of land to improve and sell in a like manner. The consequence of this way of living is that they are always moving, and their children grow up without knowing the pleasures and comforts of a home that could be made comfortable and beautiful if the land was their own, although the land can be bought very cheap. The people have been in the habit of using every man's land as their own for so many years that they have come to believe that the land has no owners. Most of the timbered lands in Eastern Texas are owned in large tracts by nonresidents, and their agents, who pay their taxes, seldom know where the land is situated; hence the squatter has it all his own way.

This timber country produces fine fruits. June apples, peaches, pears, and grapes grow to perfection when properly cultivated. At some future day fruit culture will be a source of great revenue to the people of the piney woods. The bottom land here also produces fine ribbon sugar cane, equal to any I have seen in Louisiana or elsewhere in Texas.

After a hard day's ride I stopped at a house near the road for supper and shelter for the night. About fifteen minutes after my arrival my host announced that supper was ready. I followed him from the house to the kitchen, sat down, and cast my eyes over the anticipated meal. My digestive organs, after the inspection of the supper spread before me, rebelled and contracted. The following is the bill of fare complete: cornbread, very fat bacon, and clabber. As I am not fond of clabber, I did not eat it. My host called his daughter and said: "Emma Jane, bring this man some water." The girl brought me a cup of water. My heart felt sick within me to think I could not get a cup of coffee. I had not missed my evening coffee in ten years, and the result was that I suffered a raging headache all night; and the next day the fat bacon and cornbread that I had partaken of could not or would not settle without the coffee. The next time I come along this way I will fill my pockets with ground coffee.

# WE TRAILED THEM THROUGH THE MARSHES

## BY SOLOMON ALEXANDER WRIGHT

*Solomon Alexander Wright was born in Newton County, Texas, in 1864 and died in California in 1937. The year he died he sent a longhand-written autobiography entitled* My Rambles *to J. Frank Dobie. Dobie looked it over, pronounced it "fresh and genuine" and unique in its description of life in early Southeast Texas, and published it in 1942 under the auspices of the Texas Folklore Society.*

*Solomon hunted and logged and herded and loafed all through Southeast Texas, and his journal is as casual as his life was during those last decades of the nineteenth century. Like most old-timers whose lives happen to be the East Texas big woods and the hunt, Solomon's tale is about deer, bear, and turkey hunts; water moccasins, alligators, and wild hogs; and about moving alone, slow and contented, a part of the tall timber that was so much a part of his life.*

*The following selection is from a chapter of* My Rambles *entitled "Cow Work." During those years when the West Texas ranchers were moving their herds up the prairie trails to Kansas depots, East Texas cattlemen were sifting their wild-eyed brush stock through the cypress brakes and pin-oak flats that edged the Big Thicket. They headed for the seaports of Orange, Beaumont,*

44. A brush cow coming out of the yaupon.

*and Houston, and their drives were filled with as much excitement—and boredom—as those that went up the Chisholm Trail. These drives were a part of Solomon Alexander Wright's rambles during the early 1880's.—F.E.A.*

After nearly all of the cattle were trailed out of Middle and West Texas to Wyoming and Montana, there was a mad scramble to get cattle to restock the range. As a result, stock cattle went sky high. This was in the early 'eighties. Up to that time stock cattle had been selling in East Texas for five and six dollars a head, calves thrown in. Now prices soared to fifteen dollars a head, counting calves. By "stock cattle" is meant she cattle, calves to old cows, and bulls of any age.

A Mr. Childs came from the Panhandle country down home to buy cattle, and Father sold him 150 head of scattering cattle. That is, cattle that ranged off in other people's ranges. Nearly

115

45. High water in the Big Thicket (Courtesy Clyde Gray's Heritage Garden, Woodville).

every farmer in East Texas had from half a dozen to a hundred head of cattle. Father's cattle were all Mr. Childs could buy in the lower ends of Newton and Jasper counties; so he went up country and bought about 700 head from the farmers. When he drove down to our place on his way to Orange to ship them, I got a job helping to trail them.

There is a noted swamp country in Southeast Texas called the Big Thicket. It extends west across the lower ends of Newton and Jasper counties and down into Orange County, and crosses Hardin, Liberty, Polk, Tyler, and Montgomery counties. Before it was cut off and drained, the Big Thicket was maybe fifty miles wide in places and a hundred miles long. It is low, wet, and very thick and brushy. A chain of marshes cuts it in two south of our place. The road from up country to Orange ran east of the marshes, through the Big Thicket.

Trailing nearly a thousand head of cattle down this road without losing some of them was not likely. We trailed them through the marshes. It was about ten miles through, with water six or eight inches deep. Both cattle and horses would bog about half-way to their knees every step. Here and there in the marshes are thickets of short-leaf pine saplings growing on little rises of ground. The water was not over these island plots, but the ground was full of water and was boggy enough to bog a buzzard's shadow. The first day we drove about fifteen miles to Oliver Clark's place.

Clark lived on one of those pine-sapling islands—one just high enough to afford a little drainage. His was the only habitation in the marshes that I know of. A few people lived in the Big Thicket. The only place Clark had for penning the cattle was a three- or four-acre pasture off which the timber had been cut, surrounded by a rail fence almost low enough for cattle to step over.

Childs had a chuck wagon along, and we camped at the corral and took turn about walking herd on the outside. All the cattle except the ones that had been purchased from my father were gentle farm stock. We didn't figure on any stampede and didn't need horses to keep them from stepping over the fence.

I and a puncher named Newman whom Childs had brought

down from the Panhandle were on the last watch. We were stationed on the north side of the little pasture when a little before day a thunder cloud blew up with some rain. We had put on our slickers and were keeping under a tall pine for protection against the rain. The cattle grew kind of restless, we noticed. Just before good light a sharp clap of thunder came, and they stampeded our way.

They struck the fence about forty feet from where we were, just before we could get to the place. Pulling off our slickers as we ran, we went into the stream of animals, whooping and yelling and splashing right and left with our slickers. The other boys kept them from breaking the fence anywhere else. After milling around a while, they quieted down. About fifty head got out, but they stopped and went to feeding when they got out in the marsh. That is, all but two, a cow and a yearling in Father's brand. They kept going, and I am sure they were back in their old range by night.

One year Hamp Prater bought our cattle—about four hundred head. We set out to trail them through the marshes. It had been an unusually wet spring, and the marshes were full of water. By the time we got half-way through them, the cattle were so leg-weary that it was hard to keep them traveling. Jack Wright, Blewett Thomas, and Jim Smith cut off forty head of the leaders and rushed them on ahead, with the idea that the others would string out and follow.

The wildest cattle always take the lead, and about the time we got the drags to stringing good, the lead bunch took a scare at an alligator and broke back as hard as they could run. When they ran into the main bunch, the whole herd stampeded. They tore over those islands of short-leaf pine sapling thickets, bogging to their knees but floundering on. Many of the saplings were dead, leaning over or broken off. More dangerous ground for running a horse in could hardly be imagined.

I was bringing up the drag when the stampede started, and when the cattle turned back, that put me in the lead. Stampeded cattle run in a V shape. Before I tried to circle these, I waited

46. A Thicket marsh.

until one of them took the lead and his followers formed the V. Then I dashed to the side of the leader and turned him, and kept right around with him till I ran the leaders into the tail end of the herd and got them to milling.

The other boys fell in as they came round, and we kept pressing them in until they wound up so tight they couldn't run. It didn't seem possible that that many cattle could stand on so small a piece of ground. The way they climbed up on each other, every one with his head over another's back, made the mass look like a monstrous bouquet of horns. After we got them stopped, we rode off about fifty yards and waited till they broke up and went to feeding, then started them on and didn't have any more trouble.

After we got through the marshes and struck Orange Prairie, they went along fine. About sundown we shut them up in the shipping pens. Hamp Prater set up the claim now that Father was to deliver the cattle on board the cars. There was no written agreement, Father wasn't along, and we had to stay there two days waiting for cars to load them on.

People in those days did not think of having a written agreement. At least Father didn't. Buyers would ask Father if he had sold his cattle, and if he hadn't and they agreed on a price, the buyer would ask when he could have them ready. Usually he would tell them the twentieth of June. "All right," the buyer would say, "I will be there on that day to receive them." Father never failed to have them ready and the buyer never failed to be on hand to receive them. This time in Orange was the only time there was ever a misunderstanding—or, rather, a pretended misunderstanding. Buyers generally brought the cash right along with them to pay for the cattle. A man might travel horseback alone with five or six thousand dollars.

During the spring of 1884 I was with my brother Clark Wright on Tarkington Prairie between the San Jacinto and Trinity Rivers. This was considerably west and out of the woods for me. There was so much brushy, timbered bottom country around Tarkington's Prairie that the owners of cattle there made a practice of selling off their increase at a year old. Cattle older than yearlings had a strong tendency to hide out in the swamps. The "swampers" would come out on the prairie to graze only at night. Before the owners took to selling yearlings, while they grew big steers, the cow hunters would do a big part of their work on moonlight nights. They would take advantage of the wind to ride up close to some bunch grazing, tear into them with ropes, each man roping and hog-tying his steer. The next day—sometimes not until a second or third day had come—they would drive a bunch of more or less gentle cows to where the steers were tied down, untie them, and let them loose. The steers would be so stiff from having been tied down that they could not run and would drive along.

When the time came to gather yearlings that spring of 1884, I hired out to George Allen and John Tarkington, the principal owners of cattle on Tarkington's Prairie. My brother Clark owned several hundred head, but did not have anything to do with the roundup. Frank Isaacks was boss. The hands besides myself were Frank Donahoe, John Harman, Sam Evins, Jim Booth, Walter Stetson, and Hamp Barwick. Tarkington made a regular hand, and George Allen rode some too. Chum Ritter was cook.

Allen lived on the west side of the prairie, at the edge of San Jacinto woods. The big pen was about half a mile from his house. On the north side of the pen was a clump of sweet-gum trees amid which we camped. When the gathering was over, we had about two thousand cattle under herd—about fifteen hundred yearlings, a hundred or so head of steers from two to ten years old, most of them as wild as snakes, they having got away from previous roundups, and about four hundred cows. Some of the yearlings were not weaned; we had to keep some cows, anyway, in order to be able to manage the yearlings. They were as wild as jack rabbits and could run nearly as fast.

They sold yearlings that year to a Mr. Granberry, who had a ranch near Cypress Top, southeast of Houston. He was going to drive his yearlings to that range and hold them a year or two to get the growth on them. All of the hands except Hamp and me had families, and as soon as we got the yearlings gathered, they all went home to spend the night before starting on the drive. That left only Tarkington, Isaacks, Hamp, and myself at the corral, and that was the night we had the fun.

Tarkington and I had made our beds together and were lying with our heads almost against the corral fence when, about one o'clock, the cattle stampeded. Chum Ritter, the cook, was the first one to wake. He jumped up and commenced hollering the way punchers holler to try to pacify frightened cattle. Tarkington and I both jumped up at the same time. We were about half asleep, and all we thought about was getting up a tree to keep the cattle from running over us, in case they broke the fence on our side.

I got to a tree about six inches in diameter and commenced trying to climb it. I would jump up a foot or two and slide down to the ground, and after I had made several attempts and skinned my feet pretty badly, I happened to notice Tarkington. He had got to a stump about six feet high and was trying to climb it. He would jump up a foot or two and slide down to the ground. Just as I noticed him, he jumped up and slid down and sat flat on the ground, his arms and legs locked around the stump. He looked so comical that I woke up—came to myself—and broke out in a big laugh. I imagine he thought he was eight or ten feet from the ground. But I didn't get to laugh very long. The cattle had broke through the fence on the east side, and were nearly all out of the corral and going across the prairie, hell-lickety-brendle.

We always kept a horse apiece tied up at night, in case of a stampede, and Hamp was the first one to get his horse saddled and start. I was next. When I got nearly up with the leaders, I met Hamp coming back afoot. He was riding a wild horse, and when he got nearly ahead of the cattle, his horse fell and then jerked away from him. The older steers had taken the lead. When I got up even with the leader, I dashed to his side and managed to turn him and get the herd to circling. By that time Tarkington and Isaacks got there, and we kept circling them till we ran the leaders into the tail end of the herd, got them all to milling and, finally, stopped.

By that time Allen and his boy Charlie came. They had heard the roar from their house. We headed toward Allen's pasture, about two miles away. A little after daylight we got the most of them inside. Our horses were completely played out. About a hundred cattle got away. If it hadn't been a clear night under a full moon, we'd probably not held half of them.

# TEXAS BEAR HUNT, 1906

BY A. L. KIENE

A. L. Kiene, a reporter and feature writer on the TOPEKA STATE
JOURNAL, came down to Texas and the Big Thicket in July of 1906.
On this trip he was accompanying a Santa Fe purchasing agent
who was buying poles and ties in Southeast Texas. In those days
they hunted the year around, and Kiene got in with Ben and Bud
Hooks on a summer deer and squirrel hunt. Ben killed a bear on
this hunt, and Kiene got the fever; so Ben invited him back down
for a full-scale bear hunt that winter.

The 1906 hunt that Kiene describes is a chronicle of some of the
chief bear hunters in the Thicket. Ben Hooks was Hardin County's
leading bear hunter at that time. They had struck oil on the Hooks
land in 1901, and after that Ben and Bud settled back to enjoy life.
Hunting was first on their list, and Ben Hooks' camp in the heart of
the Thicket was the starting place for many a bear and deer hunt.

Of all the old-timers who made the 1906 hunt, only Carter Hart
survives. He doesn't get around like he used to, but he can tell a
story that includes all the details of total recall. He knows a lot of
hunting tales and he tells them with an eye to accuracy and truth.
He was telling how one time he was hunting in the Hurricane,
following a course parallel to the dogs, who were taking a bear

47. A. L. Kiene (Photograph by John
Strickrott; Courtesy Thomas Sidney
Hooks).

*through the matted second growth. He said it finally got so thick
that he couldn't walk any farther, so he got up on an old downed
log that was left over from the storm that had given that area its
name. The brush had grown up on each side of the log and had
joined together at the top to form a long covered alley that a man
could crawl through. Carter headed up the log and met the bear
coming down the log from the other direction. He cut down on him
with his .44 carbine when the bear was six feet off, and the animal
hit him as it went down.*

*Benjamin Lilly was on the hunt with Kiene in 1906. Lilly was the
top bear and panther hunter in the United States then and was a
woodsman without equal. He had an uncanny sense of direction,*

48. Ben Lilly (Photograph by John Strickrott; Courtesy Thomas Sidney Hooks.)

*day or night, and couldn't be lost in any kind of woods. He lived three years in the Ben Hooks hunting camp but he always slept outside, no matter what the weather was like. The old-timers are still telling about how long he could talk without telling a lie or repeating himself, or how he could jump flat-footed out of a barrel, or how he would run a horse full gallop under a tree, grab a limb, swing up, and then climb the tree like a squirrel, chattering like one, all the way to the top. The legends of Ben Lilly are still going around in the Thicket.*

*This story was published at the time in the* Topeka State Journal. *It and the pictures are used with the permission of Thomas Sidney Hooks, Ben's son.—F.E.A.*

Kountze, Texas, December 15, 1906

The Big Thicket of Texas is known throughout the South wherever there is a man who enjoys the chase of big game. It is now recognized as one of the few refuges for the black bear, and its dense thickets and open glades furnish places and feeding grounds for the white-tail deer. There are also wild turkeys and bobcats to be found within its depths; but when anyone speaks of the Thicket now, it is always associated with bear.

The black bear of the Big Thicket is the ordinary black bear of North America. Sometimes a small full-grown bear is killed weighing as little as two hundred pounds and occasionally one that will tilt the scales at six hundred, but the average weight is probably about three hundred.

Hunting bear is great sport but it requires endurance, patience, and persistence. The writer knows more about this than he did a month ago, and he got his experience in the Big Thicket under the guiding hand of Ben and Bud Hooks, the famous bear hunters of Texas. If you leave Topeka at midnight on the Santa Fe and travel all the next day and night you will reach Kountze, Hardin County, Texas, in the heart of the Big Thicket at noon on the second day. Then hunt up the Hooks brothers and your troubles will be over so far as arrangements for the hunt are concerned. They know all about the haunts of the bear, every trail and byway of the Thicket; they own the most reliable pack of bear hounds in Texas; and what is also quite important they have a hunting lodge near the hunting grounds in the forest equipped with iron beds, mattresses and blankets. It is a two hours ride from Kountze to the Hooks' lodge. There the Kansans found two Negro cooks busily engaged in preparing supper, which on this first day consisted of bacon, sweet potatoes, warm bread, and coffee. The two cooks were Abe and Charley and they are masters of the art of preparing a meal over an open fire. In the party which gathered around the table on the first evening in camp were the two Hooks brothers; John Salters, the county clerk of Hardin County; Carter Hart, the county sur-

49. Bud Hooks and Ramsey (Photograph by John Strickrott; Courtesy Thomas Sidney Hooks).

veyor; Tom Dies, county attorney; Bill McConocoe, the sheriff; Benjamin Vernon Lilly, a veteran hunter; three men from Silsbee, Branham, Felter, and Yokes; Irving Roberts; John Strickrott, the well-known Topeka photographer; and the writer from Topeka, Kansas. During the remainder of the ten days' stay in camp there were never fewer than this number at the table and one day twenty-five people were entertained at dinner. The bill of fare was varied. Bacon was forgotten and succulent bear steaks and the juicy loin of venison were substituted.

In order to thoroughly understand how the bear in the Big Thicket are hunted and killed it is necessary to consider the two master hunters, Henry (Bud) Hooks and his brother, Ben. In this particular hunt another important factor was Benjamin V. Lilly of Louisiana, who is engaged in hunting specimens for the United

127

States biological museum and who on this occasion killed his 118th bear and let it be known that he has never had to climb a tree and has never had any hair-breadth escapes. Ben Hooks is the master of the hunt. He manages the dogs and can come nearer to keeping up with them than anyone. He is a little less than forty years old, as lithe as a greyhound, with the endurance of a well-trained athlete. He is well educated and rich, for he knew just when to dispose of his oil properties in the Beaumont fields. He lives in a beautiful home at Kountze with his family and hunts bear because he enjoys the chase. Bud, his younger brother, is heavier on his feet; he has a monstrous head covered with iron gray hair, and a ready wit. He is the life of the camp, for he is never too weary to tell a good story or enjoy a practical joke. Like his brother, he got out of "oil" in time and has the money and leisure to enjoy himself and entertain his friends. He has a charming family and his cozy home is surrounded by pens in which there are tame deer, wild geese, and a pair of year-old black bear. He is just as persistent in the chase of bruin as his older brother but is probably less often in at the death. These two men have lived in Hardin County all their lives, and if they are your friends, one of the most difficult problems of bear hunting is solved. They do not hunt for money and they would much rather give you the shot than take it themselves. They are princes in their own realm.

The bear pack is composed of Dandy, the start dog, and Ramsey, Buck, Ring, Drag, Alex, Big Foot, and Jack. Dandy is nine years old, entirely deaf, slow of motion, but still the head, the most important dog in the pack. He is a monster hound, probably containing a strain of cur. He is utterly oblivious to every track but that of the bear. He has an unfailing scent and once he strikes a trail he never quits until the bear is dead or leaves the country.

The dogs are fastened together two and two, but Dandy is allowed to roam at will. The others might chase off after a deer or bobcat but the old dog can be trusted to get what the party is hunting for. As soon as the bear leaves his bed upon the approach of the dog the rest of the pack is unleashed, and away they all go, bear and dogs, leaving Dandy far behind, still persistent with his

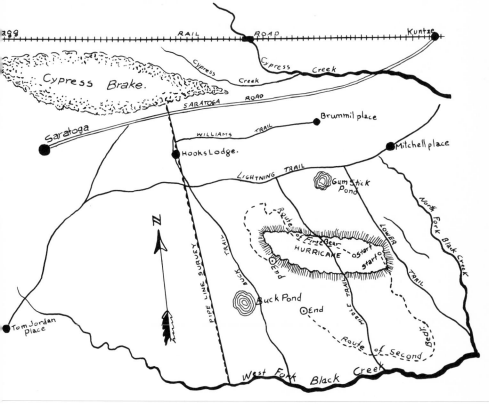

Map 3. THE HUNTING GROUNDS FOR THE 1906 HUNT (A copy made by Saul Aronow from an original drawn by Ben Hooks).

nose close to the ground, loudly baying and following as fast as his heavy legs will carry him.

While the writer was in the thicket two bears were killed. The first one was shot by Mr. Lilly in the first day's hunt after a chase of only about half an hour. The second was killed within one day of a week later. As this one more closely concerns the writer the manner of his chase and death will be told in detail.

The hunting party on this occasion was composed of ten people and eight dogs. Leaving camp at 7:30 in the morning, they took the middle trail for the bear grounds—about two miles southeast.

A trail in the Big Thicket is a path cut through the forests and tangle of underbrush and usually marked by blazed trees. It is easy enough to follow in the dense jungles, because there is no place else that will permit the free passage of a human being, but in the open forests and "burnt outs" it is often difficult to find; and once off the trail a tenderfoot is helpless.

Ben Hooks and Mr. Lilly were in charge of "the drive." The other members of the party were posted where the bear might cross the trails. The drivers, with the aid of Dandy, were supposed to find the bear and start the chase. John Salters and the writer were mounted and the rest were on foot. A horse can be ridden on the trails if the rider does not object to having his knees and shins bumped by trees, but in the thicket a horse is next to useless to one little used to riding. The men who are stationed to watch for the bear are called "standers," and this time they were scattered along the middle trail with two exceptions. Bud Hooks was stationed near the Gum Stick Pond on the Lightning Road and John Salters, who had a horse, was sent to Black Creek, four miles away. A dense undergrowth took the place of the timber and a bear may pass within ten feet of a hunter without being seen. The hunt always begins at "the Hurricane" and on this occasion Ben Hooks, Mr. Lilly, and the dogs entered the Hurricane south of the Gum Stick Pond. Then ensued a long wait while Dandy prowled through the brush in search of the track of a bear.

It was about 7:40 o'clock when the hunt began at the Hurricane, and it was nearly an hour later before Dandy lifted up his voice in the welcome though discordant notes that signaled that his quest had been successful. The trail was a hot one and in a few minutes the deep and infrequent baying of the old dog became almost a yelp, which told that the quarry had "jumped," or had left his lair. This was the signal for releasing the pack and Dandy's baying had an accompaniment which ran almost the entire gamut of dogdom.

Away they went, leaving Dandy and the drivers far in the rear. From the writer's station on the middle trail, he heard the beginning of the chase, but it was so fast and furious that the dogs were soon out of hearing. Though the writer listened intently, he was

50. Butchering the bear (Photograph by John Strickrott; Courtesy Thomas Sidney Hooks).

unable to tell which direction the dogs had gone and after waiting about a half hour he mounted his horse and rode north on middle trail to the Lightning Road; turning down toward the Gum Stick Pond he found Bud Hooks and Mr. Lilly. They did not know which way the dogs had gone, but Dandy, who had chased a cub out of the Hurricane while the pack had followed the big bear, had just returned and started south toward Black Creek. Mr. Lilly and Bud at once decided that the big bear must have gone in that direction. Mr. Lilly then gave the writer the following instructions: "Ride down to the Buck Trail and then south toward Black Creek, he may come back that way, and if he does you will meet him."

Mr. Lilly's judgment was excellent, as future developments proved. The Buck Pond was about two miles away by the trail and in that direction the tenderfoot from Kansas made his way.

The bear had run toward Black Creek just as Bud Hooks and Mr. Lilly thought, and there he encountered John Salters, a bear hunter of some distinction. The animal had stopped frequently on the way to fight the dogs, which are always troublesome though cautious, and when he had covered the three or four miles to Black Creek he was pretty well tired out. Accordingly he climbed about twenty feet up the trunk of a big pine tree, where he was safe from the dogs. Salters, from his stand, heard the dogs in the thicket and made his way toward them. There he found the bear hanging on the tree while the dogs barked spitefully below him. The hunter brought his Winchester to his shoulder and fired, and down came the bear, and the dogs at once pounced upon him. The shot was their cue. The bear was supposed to have received a mortal wound, but he shook them off, stopping only to knock one or two of them over, and again made off as fast as his legs could carry him. Salters had evidently fired too quickly or had become exhausted by his long run to the dogs, and so his aim was spoiled. The bear ran about a half a mile when he again took refuge in a tree and Salters again missed his shot. This time the bear turned north toward the Buck Pond, stopping every now and then to fight off the dogs.

When the writer reached the Buck Pond, riding slowly, he stopped, and far ahead he heard the yelping of the bear pack. At the risk of smashing a knee cap or two, he spurred the horse to a gallop. The barking came nearer and nearer. The dogs were in front of the rider, and in the thicket to the left of the Buck Trail. Tying his horse, he swung his Winchester across his arm, first making sure that there was a shell in the chamber and ran toward the thicket, where the sharp barking of the dogs indicated that the bear was at bay. When he was within a hundred yards of the place, away went the bear with the dogs at his heels, the hunter catching only a glimpse of the animal as he plunged deeper into the thicket. Following as fast as possible, the Kansan got a little nearer than before, when the bear again broke away from the dogs. He ran only a short distance and again stopped. This time the hopeful bear hunter, hot and perspiring, made a half circle; and when opposite where the dogs were barking he came in full sight of the object of

51. Playing fan-tan between hunts (Photograph by John Strickrott; Courtesy Thomas Sidney Hooks).

his search, only about thirty steps away. He was standing with his forefeet on a log and was looking back and snapping at the dogs, who were behind him at a safe distance. It was the act of a moment to bring the gun into play, and in an instant a .44-calibre Winchester ball struck the bear full in the shoulder. It was an easy shot. At the sound of the gun the dogs sprang at the animal and with a crash the dogs and bear all disappeared in the brush. Following as fast as possible, the visitor had not gone over twenty steps when back came the dogs, almost falling over each other in their hurry to escape. The hunter ran on and thirty yards farther on he almost stumbled upon the bear lying near a log and gasping his last. He had turned upon the dogs, charged, and dropped dead. It was not necessary to fire another shot. The chase was ended, but it required some time before the dogs could be induced to let the dead bear alone. They had an old grudge apparently and continued to bite the prostrate animal long after he had breathed his last.

If the tenderfoot from Kansas felt a sensation of pride, he should be forgiven, for it was his first bear. Though not naturally brave, in the excitement of the chase he had forgotten to be afraid. No thought of danger had entered his mind and the fact is that there is really little or no danger in hunting the black bear. He is always much more concerned in getting away than in inflicting bodily injury, though dogs are frequently killed. In this case not a dog was injured.

The problem that now presented itself was how to let the other men in the chase know that the end had come. Every man who hunts in the Big Thicket is equipped with a horn which is made of an ordinary steer's horn, scraped thin and with the tip end sawed off. This can be heard three or four miles after one becomes accustomed to blowing it, and it is the signal of the huntsman. Here is the code: three long blasts means "come to me"; and two blasts means "answer me"; one blast is used to call the dogs. The Kansan is not an expert at blowing a hunting horn, but he blew three blasts until it seemed as if his lips would drop off and no one answered. He fired his rifle and shouted until he was hoarse, but there was no response. Still he had no thought of leaving the bear. Bruin had assumed a position of great importance because he had permitted himself to be killed by a tenderfoot from the plains. An hour passed and then far down toward Black Creek, the deep baying of Dandy was heard. He was still following the trail of the bear that was lying dead in the thicket. The veteran hound soon came up and he forgot his age long enough to caper around the prostrate animal. This interference was resented by Buck who had curled up between the front and hind legs of the bear and who growled savagely when any other dog approached. After the bear is dead, Buck owns it—before that he seldom gets near enough to establish any claim to proprietorship.

Ten minutes after the arrival of Dandy, the hunter got an answer to his horn and shortly after the smiling face of John Salters

showed through the brush. He appeared greatly surprised and almost disgusted. "Oh, it's you, is it?" said he. "Did you kill this bear
yourself?" Then he added in a conciliatory tone. "Well, old man,
I'm mighty glad of it"; and he was.

Bud Hooks and a companion came a half hour later. They had
followed Dandy until they heard the horn.

"Which way did you run after you shot the bear?" said Bud with
a twinkle in his eye.

"Toward the course taken by the bear, of course," responded the
Kansan.

"Well these tracks don't look like it," said Bud, pretending to ex-
amine the ground. "They say that if you ran toward the bear you
ran backward."

Ben Hooks was the third arrival. He had heard the horn but ow-
ing to the difficulty with which the Kansas man sounded the sig-
nals, he had mistaken them. "I just thought it was some blamed
fool who had got lost," said he, "and I wasn't going to bother with
him until the hunt was over." There was a tone in his voice which
indicated that the man Ben thought had been lost was standing not
far away.

A trail was soon cut and the bear was put on the writer's horse,
taking his place in the saddle, and was securely tied with ropes.
The party with the bear reached camp at about 4 o'clock, after having been in the thicket for nearly nine hours without food or drink.
The actual chase of the bear occupied a little over four hours.

Dogs are seldom used for two days in succession during a bear
hunt. Unlike a deer, bruin keeps to the dense thickets when followed by dogs, and the underbrush and briars lacerate the skins of
the hounds until the dogs become too careful to be effective. They
also become foot-sore from long races. They are also often injured
by the bear. During one fight last season six dogs out of eight in the
chase were disabled by a big bear that weighed six hundred
pounds. They all recovered, however. To guard against accidents
of this kind the hunter usually empties his rifle into the bear, for it
is the wounded bear that kills and cripples dogs. The bear hunter

often delivers the death shot with the gun only a few inches from the animal's body. A bear is seldom killed by a single shot, the one captured by the writer being one of the few exceptions.

The passing of the North American black bear is only a question of a few years. The Hooks boys and their friends killed sixteen in the Big Thicket last year by persistent hunting, which was a big record. Mr. Lilly, who has spent the greater portion of his life hunting, says that there are only fifteen bear left in the Big Thicket and that there are but forty in all the southern bear territory, including Texas, Louisiana, Mississippi, and Arkansas. He does not count the Florida bear, which belong in a different class.

The Big Thicket was originally about a hundred miles long and thirty miles wide, but the axe of the lumberman has reduced it to a tract about twenty miles long and twelve or fifteen miles in width, and even now the giant pines are being felled within three-quarters of a mile of the Parker house, the hunting headquarters of the Hooks. When the forests are no more the doom of the few surviving members of the big game family in the South will have been sounded; and this time is not far away.

# BOOM-TOWN TALES

BY ALICE CASHEN


John Cashen hit town in 1904, the first year of the Batson oil boom.
He had sailed the world, starting at his home on the Isle of Man,
before he arrived, but this was his stopping place. He went to work
on the rigs, made his stake, built a house, and headed back to the
Isle of Man to take a bride.

John and Alice, the author's mother, had a hectic honeymoon.
Their ship docked at New Orleans, on their way back to Batson,
but the authorities would not let John off because his eyes looked
infected. What really happened was that he had smoked too many
wedding cigars in the cramped quarters of the ship and the smoke
had irritated his eyes. Anyhow, in spite of a long argument John
had to return with the ship to Liverpool, and Alice had to go on
alone to set up housekeeping in one of the wildest boom towns in
oil history. John signed on a freighter at Liverpool, jumped ship in
New York, and showed up broke in Batson a year later.

Alice Cashen, the author of these boom-town stories, was born
in Batson, into a part of the Big Thicket where the boomers had
ripped out a hole in the forest and planted their own kind of trees.
She grew up in a world of drill bits, bull wheels, and walking
beams, while the Batson field settled down to a quiet life as a minor
producer. The pumps are still grunting and wheezing and rocking

137

52. Alice Cashen.

*back and forth in the field north of town, but the Thicket is closing in and would spill all over it if the people ever looked the other way.*—F.E.A.

People came and went in and out of the Thicket long before the Civil War, but permanent settlements were few, and roads were even fewer. The best traveling was done on horseback, and there were times when the traveler was compelled to dismount and lead his horse through sloughs and baygalls. One of the more familiar routes was the trail between Texas and Louisiana, which led across Sam's Prairie and Batson Prairie, over which the Guedry family drove cattle to market.

One of the better known stories of this period is about a cattle rustler who managed to steal cattle while they were bedded down at night on Sam's Prairie. The drivers set a trap for him and caught him in the act of slaughtering a cow. They made him finish cleaning the carcass but had him leave the hide on. The thief was tied hand and foot, placed in the cow's carcass with his head and feet sticking out and sewed in with buckskin thongs. The owners left him to his fate. What that fate was differs with different story tellers, but imagination can furnish an end for such a thief.

The cattlemen and the rice farmers on the edges of the Thicket made only feeble efforts to conquer it, and the Thicket kept out bits of civilization—such as the cook stove, the glass windowpane, and the sewing machine—until a long time after the Civil War. Thus for a time the Thicket maintained its ominous, brooding, powerful barrier against the inroads that were to come sooner or later. The tales and stories of this area, laced together with mossy bayous and Virginia creepers, had the flavor of the wilderness and a streak of western lawlessness. To come later was a new lore unknown anywhere—oil!

On the southwest edge of the Big Thicket was the small Sour Lake settlement. The Karankawas and the Tejas had discovered this muddy lake formed by sour, acrid springs and had applied the mud successfully to sores on their skins and to granulated eyelids. Jesuit missionaries traveling from San Augustine, Florida, to San Diego, California, stopped here on the way, and it may well be that many a Sunday school was held near these springs under the Texas loblollys.

When the Mexican government granted Stephen Jackson a league of land early in the 1800's, the springs of this malaria-infested swamp were known throughout the area for their healing properties. By 1845 a cross-breed Indian and Negro had become famous for his mud baths for skin irritations. This Mr. Bazile, the self-styled Doctor Mud, was busily curing a long list of ailments with the water and mud from these springs. Some of the Sour Lake old-timers tell how Doctor Mud acquired a top hat and a dress suit too small for his gangling frame and did a thriving business in complexion packs for ladies. In 1849 other enterprising healers sunk a pipe into a promising pool of bubbles and the thick tar which oozed into the pipe was bottled and sold for twenty-five cents an ounce as a balm for rheumatism.

The fame of the springs spread. The lame, the halt, and the wrinkled came. Among these was General Sam Houston with an old leg wound. The long white Springs Hotel had many a tall Thicket tale passed around its broad verandah in the cool of the evening.

This brackish, sulphurous water brought fame of a sort to the Thicket. One Civil War tale has it that because of the blockade, in the South a shortage of sulphuric acid used for charging batteries for telegraph lines developed. Some resourceful telegraph operator tried the Sour Lake water and found it equally as effective as its commercial counterpart.

1901 roared in at Spindletop with a boom that seized the imaginations of speculators. Overnight they came, in special trains, on horseback, and in wagons; seamen left their ships in Galveston and New Orleans to rush to the mecca where a man could be broke in the morning and worth a million by night. Thousands of speculators came with maps, brochures, deeds, and abstracts, selling the same lease three or four times in one day. Land was the prize—land where water bubbled and where paraffin dirt stuck to the feet of hunters. Sour Lake seemed ideal. It had many of the qualities of the Spindletop field in addition to sour springs and gas mounds. While Spindletop was flooding the countryside with oil, speculators were scouting other likely areas. Among these speculators was "Bet-a-Million" Gates who came by private car to Sour Lake Station (now Nome), sent his agents to bargain for land at the springs, and, with the air of a man who had already made his mark, went merrily off on a quail hunt in the opposite direction.

The first well in Sour Lake was drilled by W. A. and John Savage in 1901. Others followed suit, and for three years Sour Lake, once a peaceful little spa in the Texas Thicket, became a roaring mass of oil and mud, boomers and bad men. The typical East Texas rains and the water needed for drilling made a veritable quagmire out of the entire field. Mules belly deep hitched to eight-wheel wagons were stalled for days at a time. The only way to get around the field was to walk from derrick floor to derrick floor on wooden

Oil Field.
Saratoga-Texas-

53. The Saratoga oil field (Courtesy Clyde Gray's Heritage Garden, Woodville).

boards. This was easily done because leases, sometimes one-twentieth of an acre, were so small that owners were barely able to set their rigs up in their allotted spaces, and derricks stood leg-to-leg, back and forth across the field which was later to become the birthplace of the now famous Texas Company. Masses of humanity worked, slept, and ate in this pandemonium with no thought of anything except getting rich. Beds were rented by the hour; meals were cooked in canvas cafes, and one enterprising saloonkeeper rushed into town with six bottles of whiskey, swiped a rived board from a corn crib, nailed it between two trees, and Sour Lake's Big Buck Saloon was in business. The boom spread, and the Thicket was due to suffer another oil invasion a year later in Saratoga.

Saratoga is credited with being the second oil strike in the Thicket, but oil activity of a sort had begun there much earlier than anywhere else in Texas. In 1867 an Alabama Indian offered a nest-

141

er a bottle of thick, black oil. The native refused that offer. The Indian then offered to lead the prospect to the oil spring for $25.00. Word soon spread about the bottle of oil, and Fletcher Cotton, noticing that his hogs always came out of a certain part of the Thicket slick and glossy, followed them and discovered a stinking slough of bubbles. He drove a two-inch pipe into the pond, waited, and after a while oil rose in the pipe. Others heard this tale, and, taking a leaf out of the Sour Lake book, the natives built a bath house over the springs and borrowed the name of the famous New York Saratoga Springs. For many years these springs attracted visitors with ulcers and arthritis, but since few "cures" were permanent, Saratoga never became a health resort, and buildings eventually were allowed to tumble down. The Thicket was moving in again on the sulphur springs when the oil field roared in.

On the strength of his experiment with the pipe, Cotton made the first oil agreement in the Thicket when he leased a tract of land to a Von Hartin who drilled a shallow, unsuccessful well in 1881, fully twenty years before Spindletop. In 1903, two years after Spindletop, the Hooks Brothers of Kountze drilled the first producing well. They were not professional speculators, and they sold out and retired after the first hole.

The Saratoga boom was explosive, following the pattern of the Sour Lake and Spindletop strikes. The presence of a railroad made the town accessible to outsiders, and they came in droves, bringing with them all the daring, lawlessness, and greed that characterized booms. There is no way to estimate the extent of crime that rode in with every boom, but those who can remember say there was plenty of it, and Saratoga soon had a rival boom town nearby where oil invaded the Thicket for the third time in Batson. The Thicket wildcat was meeting his match in a new breed—the Wildcatter—who made his predatory way through the bobcat dens searching for a new kind of treasure.

There had long been signs of oil on Sam's Prairie, a vast burned off saucer where tall grass grew after a roaring fire. At the tiny Otto postoffice, some twenty families called weekly for mail. Asphalt pits and oil seeps were easily fired by passing cattlemen. Crawdad holes blew gentle bubbles after rains, and a sour-sweet smell crept low over the prairie when clouds were heavy. Almost daily prospectors got off the train at the Saratoga depot, caught a local hack, crossed Pine Island Bayou, and asked the way to these freaks of nature.

One morning a local hack driver hauling the mail met Steve Pipkin, a prospector from Beaumont, who asked for a guide to the bubbling slough. The driver took him to Knight's Cove—too dry at the time to emit bubbles. Pipkin broke off a persimmon limb and began to make holes in the mud a few inches deep. Out of his pocket he took a small tomato can, cut the side and top, and fashioned a crude funnel which he placed over one of the mudholes. After banking it well with mud, he struck a match and held it to the small end of the inverted funnel. Nothing happened. He asked the driver to come close to see if he could observe anything. Pipkin held his finger over the hole for a few seconds and applied a second match; this time the driver jerked back because there was a brief flare. The hack driver's next assignment was to take his fare to the owner of the land, a nester who had little interest in anything other than hogs, cattle, and farming. After a few simple negotiations, Pipkin agreed to pay $85,000 for the 160 acres. Trusting nobody, the nester demanded his pay in cash, which was counted out into his wife's calico apron by a friend to whom he paid $10,000 for this chore and for delivering the money to a Liberty bank. This was the beginning of what later became the Paraffine Oil Company.

A few weeks later the Thicket dwellers were shaken to their toes by the rumble of the Paraffine discovery well. It was a gusher at 790 feet with an initial production of six hundred barrels per day. The boom erupted, upsetting, for the third time, the whole way of life in the Thicket. Salt water and thick black scum crept over the pastures and contaminated the bayous. Escaping gas was insidious and was flared for safety's sake, lighting the woods and driving off game. Nesters resented this and had ingenious ways of getting even with the roughnecks. Because of the terrain, the only possible way for the driller and his crew to get to work was on horseback. They tied their horses in the shade a distance from the rig and left them all day. One astonished crew found their horses daubed with assorted colors of barn paint by indignant natives who hated oil in any form. Night watchmen were posted on rigs because the natives took a very dim view of this so-called "progress."

Batson was the third salt dome after Spindletop, and it seemed that the first fields were only preludes to the swelling acts of lawlessness which came later to this town. On they came—speculators, gamblers, boomers, honest men, and lechers—on horseback, on muleback, with ox teams and wagons. When the mud got too deep, they laid logs across it and called the result a "corduroy" road. Equipment was pulled in by mules and ox teams, four and eight up. Saloons, gambling houses, cafes, and so-called "hotels" soon pushed up gaudy false fronts along a street called Fannin after its counterpart in Beaumont. Ragtown stretched into the field, and tents, trees, and arbors served as shelters to men who gave little time to sleep. Boardinghouses sprang up at intervals between town and the field and later were connected to these by a boardwalk built some two feet above mud and mire.

Lawlessness was the ordinary way of life. Kountze was the county seat, and prisoners were hauled there in wagons, but as time went on, there were not enough wagons, and prisoners were chained to trees and left until they could be picked up. Later a makeshift, one-room jail which obviously couldn't keep a rabbit caged, was built. Here, by a sort of gentleman's agreement, some prisoners served their time for drinking or fighting. One hearty was observed outside whitewashing the jail one afternoon.

"What in the hell are ya doin' that fer, Ed?" asked a passerby.

"Wal, I spen' so much o' m' time hyar, I jest figgered I'd clean it up a little."

Lawlessness increased with the increase in production. By this time Batson was producing more oil per day than Sour Lake or Spindletop. Fights were common on the streets, and shooting scrapes were far too frequent. One dandy who had become affluent overnight prided himself on his fancy attire. His pride and joy was a pair of gaudy suspenders. He had gained a reputation as a gun fighter, and most of the boomers were afraid of him. One day in a

54. A Batson prisoner (Courtesy Clyde Gray's Heritage Garden, Woodville).

saloon he got into an argument and dared his adversary into the
street. This adversary stood some forty feet in front of the swinging doors and called to the dandy. Out he came reaching for the
gun which he was never able to draw. As he slumped against a
post, he gasped, "It hung in my suspenders—I didn't have a
chance." Dr. John Bevil, who now lives in Beaumont, picked him
up and took him to the drug store where he died.

Even the so-called law in Batson was lawless. The justice of the
peace had a system of fines. His arrangement was simple for him
as well as the lawbreakers. He would hail all gamblers and shady
ladies into court every Monday morning where they would pay
fines and return to business immediately. The size of the fine sometimes depended upon the need of the J.P. Once, when he wanted
to take his lady to the St. Louis Fair, the fines were tripled.

Fannin Street was the backdrop for an assortment of characters fit for any fiction. Straw Hat Kate kept a wealthy local oil man busy every afternoon for six months teaching her how to ride a new red bicycle behind the Blue Front Saloon. Coal Oil Katy kept the lamps polished in a local "hotel" and was often saturated with oily soot and smut, which gave her her name.

The Batson boom had also attracted some "furriners," who brought with them the enmities and loyalties of other days. Among the independent oil producers were an Irishman and a Manxman who bunked together and wildcatted together. A small Irish Rebellion erupted annually on St. Patrick's Day when the Irishman flew the green flag of Southern Ireland above the crown block of the highest derrick, and on March 18th the Manxman retaliated by running up the orange flag of Northern Ireland in its place.

Out of such a conglomeration of humanity as gathered in boom towns must come all sorts of tales. Many of these are about roustabouts, pumpers, teamsters, and loafers, but one of them deals with the gentler type. Such a one was the owner of the first real confectionery in Batson. He brought in a marble soda fountain that was the wonder of the town. Circular tables with curled iron chairs added elegance to an establishment that immediately became popular. However, this quiet, self-effacing man was to have his test. Between serving sodas, he sat crocheting dainty baby shoes, caps, and doilies. For several weeks he kept this up and paid no attention to the coarse comments that some of the local roughnecks were making. One evening four drunks dared one of their members to go to the confectionery and bring the crocheting back and hang it on the bar. The toughest member of the crew strode into the confectionery and demanded the handiwork. The dark, brooding Spaniard methodically wound up his thread, set it on the fountain, let go with a right, and the surprised roughneck found himself half in and half out of the confectionery. He picked himself up and went back to his cronies. The Spaniard never had any trouble after that as he busily turned out his lace.

The greenhorn tale is found in all industry, but it was probably more pronounced in the early days of oil because most oil men

146

55. Boilers and men (Courtesy Clyde Gray's Heritage Garden, Woodville).

were beginners. The typical greenhorn story is usually about the
unfortunate beginner who was sent for the "pipe stretchers," "the
sky hook," "the dead man," and the "wire winder." Many a poor
novice was sent from lease to lease inquiring for a mythical piece
of equipment until he was the laughingstock of the whole town.

Ingenious use was made of oil-field machinery, and the pumpers
found the "blowout" box especially useful. This was a large box
where steam from boilers was released under pressure. When it
was necessary to lower boiler pressure, the blowout box served as
a baffle. This was ideal for cleaning oil-soaked overalls and even
hats, which would come out battered but immaculately clean. After work, the roughnecks would bathe, put on clean clothes, leaving their mud-caked overalls on the floor, and, consequently, the
bath house always smelled like anything but roses. When the

147

56. Oil well and crew working for Miss Cashen's father (Courtesy Clyde Gray's Heritage Garden, Woodville).

57. A palmetto shack, Batson (Courtesy Clyde Gray's Heritage Garden, Woodville).

pumper came to work, he often found piles of filthy clothes with instructions to throw them into the blowout box and hang them on the nearest barbed wire fence. Eventually, one pumper sought revenge. This crafty fellow bought ten packages of Putnam's turkey red dye and included it in his next wash. That particular gang pulled wells in pink overalls for a long time after that. Hats suffered also. Felt, after a session in the blowoff box, was pliable in the hands of an imaginative pumper who stuck a two-foot stick into the crown to produce an oil-field version of the dunce cap. Another resourceful pumper placed thin slivers of limburger cheese in the sweatbands of the roustabouts' hats, and watched their consternation as the temperature rose.

The native courtesy of the Thicket often carried over into oil-field practice. A stranger was never asked his full name because he might not take kindly to an inquiry so personal. Usually Thicket names found their way into oil fields. Indian Joe was a teamster; the Big Thicket Kid was a bartender; the Notchcutter was a log-house builder; Buckskin Joe rode a buckskin horse, and Broom Face was a man who had no love for barbers. Hambone Duty was the name of a part-Indian derrick man. Late one afternoon Hambone was up on the thribble board high in the derrick when the pipe stuck. The driller put all the power of the rig into pulling the pipe out of the hole. The derrick strained and cracked, and Hambone held on. The legs of the derrick began to give way. Hambone shouted, but there was no time for the crew to do anything but run for their lives or be crushed by heavy derrick timbers. Down came the derrick with Hambone on it! The crew rushed in to see what must be tragedy. There was a gurgle and a mud-encrusted figure squirmed in the slush pit until timbers could be lifted. Hambone was hastily dragged from the pit, while he clutched frantically at the left side of his chest. He clawed open the watch pocket of his overalls and pulled out a piece of paper.

"Thank Gawd," said Ham, "I thought I'd lost Jim's poker IOU."

Another pumper story is about a rotund pumper named Dimp, who later became a millionaire. He always went to work the evening "tower" (tour) with his twelve deer hounds and his rifle. He

58. An oil well burning (Courtesy Clyde Gray's Heritage Garden, Woodville)

59. A Batson street scene (Courtesy Clyde Gray's Heritage Garden, Woodville

60. Hauling drilling equipment (Courtesy Mrs. Aline House).

was the nervous type who recognized the lawlessness of a boom town. It was a cold night. The boilers were under a full head of steam. The boilerhouse was new, and the door had been merely propped against the opening as protection against a bitter north wind. Dimp and his dogs were dozing peacefully when—bang! The wind blew the noisy tin door against the boilerhouse and pandemonium broke loose. Dimp dropped his gun; it went off and shot a hole in the boiler, and steam roared and hissed. The dogs ran in every direction, and so did Dimp. He told the story on himself and said that he found himself and the dogs half a mile away from the boilerhouse sitting by the road panting on a cold night. This story has several versions which include Dimp's being fired the next day.

Decent women seldom figure in oil-field folklore, but there is one Batson story that will bear telling about a lady innocent abroad. An Englishman working in Batson invited his sister to visit him. Fresh from Liverpool, this genteel young lady was ready to see the wide new world. One afternoon while her brother was

151

61. The Batson auction: periodically these ladies were auctioned off to the highest bidders—not for keeps, however (Courtesy Clyde Gray's Heritage Garden, Woodville).

working, she dressed in her best—pink umbrella, pink hat, high-top black-and-white shoes—and went to town for a soda. She picked her way through the mud and brush and finally reached the new sidewalk that led right past the nine saloons. She chose the first at hand, made her way through the greasy roughnecks having their usuals, and sat down at a vacant table. A strange stillness came over the room. Perhaps a look at a decent young lady took the boomers back to some distant days before they came to Batson. The bartender came around the bar and asked what she would have. "A strawberry soda, please." Silence again fell over the bar. Never at a loss, the bartender sent a boy out the back door and down the street to the drugstore where sodas were served to bring back a double strawberry concoction. The young lady took her time, obviously enjoyed her drink, and left, thanking the bartender. After her exit, a guffaw that filled that end of town rolled from the swinging doors, and another bit of boomer folklore was born.

Merchants had their troubles with boomers too. One Jewish vendor sat among his piles of overalls and workshoes and managed to do well even in the face of the necessity of doing a credit business at times. He soon learned those he could depend upon to come around on payday and those who were not so reliable. His favorite tid-bit was pickled pig's feet. These he nibbled constantly, always careful to hide the fact from the public in general, and from his very religious wife in particular. His sense of humor and his desire to prosper were evident when he told about selling a pair of shoes to the town deadbeat. This man was shopping for a gift for a lady in one of the "hotels" down the street. Since these ladies seldom left their places of business, it was perfectly logical that her friend should shop for her. The boomer selected a pair of shoes, hesitated awhile, and finally asked that he be allowed to take the shoes to the hotel to see if they were what the lady liked. He would then return and pay for the shoes or return them if they were not satisfactory. The canny merchant wished fervently for a sale; but, remembering the deadbeat's reputation, he was in a quandary. He finally consented to let the boomer give the lady a choice. He took a box— carefully wrapped it and handed it to the boomer.

153

His wife, watching the procedure, was indignant. "Why did you do that? You will never see him again!"

Abe answered, "Oh yess, I vill. Into dat box I put two shoes for de von foot!"

The boomer soon returned, called attention to the fact that there were two left shoes, paid for the pair, and left.

The Rangers came and dealt with the law as well as the lawless. They helped the local citizens to clean up the town. Respectable people were safe on the streets, and oil became an industry instead of a bonanza. Producers made attempts to curb the salt water and oil residue that desolated the Thicket on the west side. The Gulf Oil Company built houses for its employees, and the people were encouraged to build schools and support churches. The wilder element of the town seemed to drift away in time, and Batson settled down, as did Saratoga and Sour Lake, into a peaceful humdrum of ordinary life.

The tired little towns nestle close to the Thicket like spent old boomers who doze in the still East Texas afternoons and dream of new fantastic leases where gushers roar over the tops of derricks and the world is wild again in a frenzy for oil. Oil tales are spun in elegant petroleum clubs; old-timers recall vivid pictures of boom towns seething with humanity. Into these accounts the flavor and color of Thicket oil fields—Sour Lake, Saratoga, and Batson—will always creep. Spindletop was the birthplace of the oil industry, but the Big Thicket was its cradle.

# TALES FROM UNCLE OWEN

BY LOIS WILLIAMS PARKER

The end of the Civil War was the end of Andrew Jackson Williams
as a small plantation owner in Alabama. He was fifty years old in
1865 and past the time in life when a man usually thinks about
making a fresh start. But his part of Alabama was a waste, and
there was nothing to do but to see what could be made of what was
left in life. The family, which included six children and one on the
way, sailed from Mobile to Southeast Texas in the early fall of
1865 and built their first house in the Big Thicket on the bank of
Steep Bank Creek.

    The Williams just naturally took to sawmilling in the Thicket.
Jackson had done some lumbering in Alabama, and his sons—
Dave, Jep, and Owen—took up where he left off, rafting logs down
Village Creek and the Neches to the Beaumont mills. By the turn
of the century they were prospering lumbermen, furnishing tim-
bers for the rigs and plank roads of the Saratoga, Batson, and Sour
Lake oil fields. Dave opened his big mill in 1904. The location was
first known as Williams' Station, but because there was another
Williams, Texas, the name was changed to Thicket.

    Dave and his son Lee operated sawmills all over the Big Thick-
et. Uncle Owen worked with them for many years as a sawyer, but
he leaned more to socializing and politicking than to fighting saw
logs.

    Some tales were told on Uncle Owen, too. They say that when

155

62. Lois Williams Parker.

*he was running for state representative, the main plank in his plat-*
*form was a promise to get the dates of the squirrel season changed*
*for the Big Thicket district. When he finally got his bill passed in*
*Austin he felt that he had accomplished his political purpose, so he*
*didn't run again. And then there was the time when he was the*
*deputy sheriff and heard that a Negro bootlegger was getting off*
*the train at Bragg Station with a suitcase load of shinny. Uncle*
*Owen was there to meet him and he quickly told the big Negro*
*that law had him. Something went wrong, however, between the*
*"You're under arrest" and the handcuffing, and the next thing Un-*
*cle Owen knew he was lying on the ground by the tracks, looking*
*into the syrup-bucket-size barrel of his own .44. The bootlegger*
*gave him a good cussing and then took Uncle Owen's boots and*
*his horse and headed into the woods to peddle his moonshine.*
*Uncle Owen had a long, barefooted walk back to Honey Island.*

    *Lois Williams Parker, the author of "Tales from Uncle Owen,"*
*was Lee's daughter and Owen's great niece, and as such grew up in*
*the Thicket to the musical accompaniment of a mill whistle and a*
*circle saw.—F.E.A.*

63. Uncle Owen on the gallery (Courtesy Lois Williams Parker).

Uncle Owen was the depot agent at Honey Island in the Big Thicket; he was also deputy sheriff and district representative to the state legislature. Besides that, he was the justice of the peace and notary public, a Baptist, and a Mason. A good percentage of the Hardin County population were his nieces and nephews, and to 99 percent of the people he was Uncle Owen. To the other one percent he was W. O.

It was a rare night in my childhood when we didn't walk down to Uncle Owen's after supper. In the summer, spring, or fall, and all but the coldest nights of winter, we sat on the front gallery. My own sharpest memories of these occasions are Uncle Owen's accounts of the happenings of the day in Honey Island. Some were not meant for my ears, but these are the ones that I heard most distinctly and remembered the longest, despite the low talk and whispers. It was easy to need a drink of water if Daddy and Uncle Owen were talking near the end of the gallery where the bucket and dipper were. A lot of funny things happened in Honey Island, to hear him tell it.

In those days before radio, the arrival of the morning train brought the news of the world in the *Beaumont Enterprise*. Uncle Owen could hardly wait to close up the depot and get home to drink the coffee he knew Aunt Min would have waiting and to read and enjoy the daily news. He always read the front page while he was walking home. One morning when the train came and brought the *Enterprise*, the headline blared the news of President Warren G. Harding's death. Uncle Owen walked hurriedly home to tell Aunt Min the news. Just as he reached his front gate, Mr. Nicholbur rounded the bend in his wagon; he was bringing in some produce to swap at the commissary for sugar, coffee, and tobacco. Uncle Owen waited, eager to break the news to Mr. Nicholbur. When Mr. Nicholbur saw Uncle Owen, he slowed and stopped the team. Uncle Owen called to him, all the while waving the paper and leaving off preliminary greetings.

"Harding is dead, Nicholbur! Harding is dead!"

Mr. Nicholbur sat very still for a moment, shaking his head without comment. It was obvious that he was disturbed. Finally he spoke: "Now who do you suppose will sell us the medicine?"

Walking on over closer to the wagon, Uncle Owen asked, "What do you think I said, Nicholbur? I said that the President of the United States, President Harding, is dead."

Mr. Nicholbur brightened. "Why W. O., I thought you meant Mr. Hardin, the Watkins man, and it really took me back. Too bad about the President, but I'm sure powerful glad it wasn't Mr. Hardin, the Watkins man. Giddap!"

Then there was the day that Uncle Owen went into the commissary to get a plug of Brown Mule. After Mr. Douglas cut it off, sacked it, and handed it to him, Uncle Owen took out his pocket-knife and cut himself a chew while waiting for Mr. Douglas to weigh up a couple of pounds of peaberry coffee for Bud Hendrix. After Bud got his coffee he and Uncle Owen sauntered on toward the door, finishing up a bit of conversation.

In the meantime, Mrs. Powers had come into the drygoods side of the commissary and settled her huge bulk down in a chair in the shoe department.

"No need to measure for size, Mr. Douglas. It's a 9B and I want a low-quarter shoe with a thick, extension sole if you've got it."

Mr. Douglas selected a box from the shelves and returned and straddled the shoe stool in front of the big woman, who had already removed her left shoe and placed her foot on the incline of the stool. He carefully picked up her foot and began pushing on the shoe while she looked all around the store, unconscious of the shoe-trying process. Mr. Douglas reached in his hip pocket for his shoe horn so he could speed up the operation. And Uncle Owen and Bud Hendrix stopped even with the shoe department to talk about county politics. Both of them happened to look in Mr. Douglas' direction just as he leaned over to insert the shoe horn and put some more pressure on the heel. Mrs. Powers, who had been concerned only with her surroundings to the right and to the left and over her head, now looked down over her tremendous bosom to see the new shoe. A look of horror came over her face. Seeing Mr. Douglas' very bald head in front of her, she mistook it for her bare knee and quickly lifted her big floral skirt to cover it. Mr. Douglas finally unwound himself, while Uncle Owen and Bud Hendrix looked on. According to Uncle Owen, Mr. Douglas' big nose was "redder than ary bell pepper you ever saw," and it was this very incident that prompted the hiring of Hobart Hill as the drygoods clerk.

One day the morning passenger train pulled in and nobody got off but a drummer who had come to call on the commissary manager. You didn't have to ask if he was a drummer. It was obvious by his sample case, which was not shaped like an ordinary grip; it was longer and narrower and thinner. Right away it was obvious

64. A baptizing near Saratoga (Courtesy Clyde Gray's Heritage Garden, Woodville).

also that you weren't going to have a chance to do any asking because he was going to do it all.

He addressed Uncle Owen. "What time now did this train arrive, and when is the next one out? Just how deep is that mill pond, mister, and I wonder if you can tell me how that Dago sells his bananas?"

Uncle Owen looked at him coldly and answered:
"In at eight,
Out at nine,
Up to your rump,
Three for a dime."

As justice of the peace, Uncle Owen performed lots of marriage ceremonies. I remember when Lige and Matilda got married. Lige was never thought to be very bright, which might be accounted for by the fact that he lisped and had crossed eyes. But Lige was a hard worker at the sawmill, where he rolled dollies of lumber all day long.

One Saturday afternoon Uncle Owen and Aunt Min were sitting on the front gallery when Lige drove up in his Model T. He was all dressed up in a blue serge suit. Matilda sat beside him in a shiny Copenhagen blue dress. Uncle Owen called "Come in," and both got out.

Lige pulled out a legal-looking paper from his hip pocket and handing it to Uncle Owen, he explained that he and Matilda wanted to be married. Uncle Owen told him that he ought to have brought along some witnesses, but then they hollered across to the planer mill and Charley Sharp walked over. He and Aunt Min witnessed the ceremony. After proudly kissing his new bride, Lige pulled a twenty-dollar bill from his pocket and offered it to Uncle Owen. Uncle Owen refused it, saying that the usual fee was only three dollars, and "I wouldn't charge you anything at all, Lige."

Lige insisted a while longer, and wouldn't leave until Uncle Owen told him to get some change at his own convenience and come back and pay him.

The newlyweds didn't go out of town, because Lige had to go back to work Monday. In fact, it had taken some doing for him to get off for his wedding Saturday.

Sunday morning bright and early Lige was back at Uncle Owen's, tapping on the gallery with his fist. Uncle Owen peeped out and saw it was Lige, so he went to the door in his nightshirt.

"Now lithen here, Uncle Owen," Lige said: "I want you to take thith here twenty dollarth. It wath wuth it!"

Uncle Owen took his money.

Brother Hammond was the only preacher at the community church house in Honey Island for a mighty long time. There was baptizing in the millpond regularly, dinner on the ground every fifth Sunday, services morning and evening every Sunday, and a prayer meeting every Wednesday night. Brother Hammond preached the plain gospel without any frills or furbelows, and he

161

65. Big Thicket sawmills(Courtesy Thomas Sidney Hooks).

didn't feel that he needed any fancy education to interpret the Book.

Then a young fellow by the name of Spratt, who was fresh out of some sort of off-brand religious school, barged in on Brother Hammond's congregation. He challenged Brother Hammond to a debate on one of his own favorite subjects, the doctrine of baptism and total immersion. Brother Hammond had no doubts about the necessity and power of total immersion, and he didn't feel this young sprout was worth his time, but since Mr. Spratt had bawled out loud in front of two of his most likely converts, he felt compelled to answer him. It was decided that they would meet for the debate that very Sunday afternoon.

The sinners as well as the saints gathered at the church for this occasion, for this sort of thing didn't take place every Sunday in Honey Island. Mr. Spratt was up first to state his cause against total immersion. He read scripture and expounded. He reasoned and quoted poetry. He told funny stories to illustrate his point. He talked without ceasing for two hours and forty minutes and wound up his argument by beseeching his Maker to help Brother Hammond see the error of his ways. It was a fine talk and everybody got a big kick out of it, but of course they couldn't clap.

Then Brother Hammond took the floor. "Brothers and sisters," he said, "I want you to turn with me to the twenty-second chapter of the Book of Acts, verse sixteen, and read with me. 'And now why tarriest thou? Arise and be baptized and wash away thy sins, calling on the name of the Lord'." Brother Hammond sat down.

Young Spratt was greatly surprised and taken aback by so short a speech. For a moment he acted as though he wasn't going to get up for his next round, but he did. And he talked and he talked, explaining and expounding against the doctrine of baptism for another forty-five minutes before he sat down again.

Brother Hammond rose to his feet for the rebuttal. "Brothers and sisters, it's still thar. 'And now why tarriest thou? Arise and be baptized and wash away thy sins'."

The two prospective converts walked right up and gave Brother

163

Hammond their hands and Jesus their hearts, and there was a baptizing by total immersion on the millpond without further delay. This was followed by a general session of merry-making to the Lord. Mr. Spratt left and nobody ever heard of him again.

Uncle Owen often rode the Thicket and just visited people even when he wasn't running for anything. Many of the people of the Thicket were very poor, but they were generous hearted. There were the Larkins, who had a large family and not much of a farm, but they made a living. Uncle Owen stopped by one day. All of the family were glad to see him, and nothing would do but he stay for dinner. They sat down to a large mess of collards on a right big platter, a plate filled with squares of cornbread, and a noticeably small dish of Irish potatoes.

After returning thanks, Mr. Larkin passed the cornbread to Uncle Owen. Then he passed the plentiful platter of collard greens and Uncle Owen helped himself. Then he passed the rather smallish dish of Irish potatoes. Uncle Owen took only a very small portion, knowing that it had to go around.

Mr. Larkin noticed this immediately and insisted, "Please take more, Uncle Owen. Take nearly all of 'em."

Uncle Owen and Aunt Min frequently went to the play parties given about the area. They liked to watch the young people dance Josey, and if there was fiddling going on, they enjoyed that because both of them played the fiddle after a fashion. The night the Roaches had the play party for Feenie, it had already been noised around that they were going to have ice-cold lemonade with the birthday cake. Somebody had seen Dester Crosby driving his ice truck out in that direction. Mr. Crosby brought ice from Kountze to the Honey Island commissary every other day, and Mr. Roach had left word that he would pay a little extra if Mr. Crosby would make a delivery right to his house.

This was Feenie's sixteenth birthday, and she was the Roaches only child, which was unusual and a circumstance often pitied in the Thicket. The Roaches were anxious to sort of put on the dog since this was like a coming-out party for Feenie.

That night the folks gathered from all around about and everybody was having a good time. Even some of the old folks who hadn't fleshened up too much were out in the dog trot cutting the seed collard. About ten-thirty most folks' mouths were watering for some of that ice-cold lemonade and layer cake. So Mr. Roach went over to the big square-dug well, where the butter and milk were hung to keep them cool. He leaned over the curb, got hold of a well rope that hung over the side, and gave a hard pull. Nothing pulled back. He sat down flat on the ground and a big loop on the other end flopped out of the well and landed square dab around his neck.

"Now, by gravy, what do you reckon went with that hunnert pounds of ice?" he asked.

Anyway, the well water was a bit cooler than usual and the weather was hot and most of the folks weren't used to ice-cold lemonade in the first place.

Honey Island didn't have a regular preacher before Brother Hammond settled there. Brother Teal from over Saratoga way came about once a month and held service. He usually spent Sunday night with some of the congregation. The mill foreman, Paul Palmer, and his wife invited him on one occasion to spend the night with them. When they got over to the Palmer's house that night, Mrs. Palmer went over and picked up the Bible, and called the family together for the reading of a few verses and a family prayer before going to bed. Brother Teal commented that this sort of thing was always done in the old days, but in these hurried sawmill days it was about to become a thing of the past. Mrs. Palmer, getting in the mood of the discussion and wanting to seem especially pious, volunteered that it was a practice that her family always observed. Brother Teal looked at the Bible and thought that they sure had kept it new looking using it every night. He commented on what a handsome book it was and asked how long they had had it.

66. Sunnydale Church.

"Seventeen years," said Mrs. Palmer. "It was a wedding present from my sainted mother," she added.

Brother Teal left the next day and didn't return to Honey Island for another month. On his next visit, he deliberately got himself invited to the Palmer's again, this time just for Sunday dinner.

67. Sunnydale Church.

Just before dinner was called, when all the men were sitting on the front gallery, Brother Teal went over and washed his face in the washpan, dried leisurely on the towel that hung nearby on a nail, and reached for the comb which lay on a small shelf beneath the mirror.

"Well, I see you have a new comb," Brother Teal remarked.

"Yes, we lost the other one and never could find it," Mrs. Palmer answered as she poked her head out the door to say that dinner was on the table.

After dinner Brother Teal and the family went into the front room, and Brother Teal stretched himself out on the duofold and looked up at the ceiling and started talking about what a great book the Bible was. Then he asked Mr. Palmer if he knew what kind of razor the Lord shaved with. Mr. Palmer didn't know and Brother Teal didn't tell him. Then he asked Mrs. Palmer what St. John saw when the seventh seal was broken. Mrs. Palmer didn't know. Neither of them knew who lapped water like a dog either; so Brother Teal asked Mrs. Palmer to hand him their Bible, which was on the library table near her. He took the book, opened it up, and out fell the comb that had been lost a month.

"Now I remember," said Brother Teal; "I put that comb in there the last time I was here to mark my place."

167

One night it was cold as floogins and we were down at Uncle Owen's listening to him tell about that stormy night that he got lost near the old haunted Haney place. Dr. Swearingen was new there at Honey Island then. Sometimes he got lonesome and he'd come down, like tonight, and sit with us at Uncle Owen's. About the time the story got interesting, we heard someone call, "Hello," at the back door.

"That's old Uncle Alex," Uncle Owen said, recognizing his voice. "I guess there's some trouble over in the quarters." But what Uncle Alex really wanted was to see Dr. Swearingen.

"Ah wants you to give me anotha one o' dem pieces o' papah, Doctah," Uncle Alex said, after Uncle Owen had brought him in out of the cold.

"You mean another prescription?" Dr. Swearingen asked.

"Yassuh," Uncle Alex answered. "Dat las' one sho' did do de ole' 'oman good. Ah rubbed it on her laigs jest lak you tole me and it hope her a heap, but dat piece o' papah done plum wo' out, and dat's why ah done had to come fo' anothah."

Dr. Swearingen was on his feet in a split second and was reaching for his hat. "Uncle Alex, you come right on up to my office and I'm going to change the treatment. I have something there that will do even more good than that prescription."

"Yassuh," said Uncle Alex as he followed him on out.

When they were out of hearing, Uncle Owen looked over at Aunt Min and said, "Folks here in Honey Island sure are lucky to have Dr. Swearingen's services—black or white."

# SOUR LAKE: Spa of the Big Thicket

BY RUTH GARRISON SCURLOCK

*Ruth Scurlock, as a teacher and professional writer-journalist, has been covering the stories of East Texas and the Big Thicket since the late 'twenties. She wrote about and participated in many of the early attempts to establish parts of the Thicket as game and forest conservation areas and collaborated with Dean Tevis in feature writing the best of the East Texas editions of the BEAUMONT ENTERPRISE.*

*The Sour Lake that Ruth writes about was a watering place from the beginning, when the Indians first decided that any water that smelled and tasted that bad ought to be good for them. And it was a prospering community at the turn of the century. Then came the oil boom in 1901 and the whole tenor of the town changed. Sour Lake became the political hub of Hardin County for a while and had three newspapers to boast of its accomplish·ments, one of which was giving birth to the Texas Company.*

*One of the most interesting episodes in Sour Lake oil history occurred in 1929. Early on the morning of October 9, a Texas Company man noticed that a piece of company land about two hundred feet across was sinking and had already sunk about fifteen feet below its normal level. Two sweet-gum trees stood in the sink area, and as the man watched he could see them slowly*

169

68. Ruth Garrison Scurlock.

*going down. A little over an hour later the sink was fifty feet deep and the sides were beginning to crack. By noon the sink was ninety feet deep and was filling with mud, sand, water, and oil. All of this caused excitement and speculation, and as the story of the sink was retold it grew into legendary proportions, with men, mules, and machinery going very dramatically down the hole. More objective reports indicate that besides the land, only a boiler was lost—and the two sweet-gum trees, both sunk completely out of sight. The geologists' diagnosis was that a cavity filled with liquids and sands had been pumped clean by twenty-eight years of continual pumping, and that the crust had fallen in. The Sour Lake Sink is not much to look at now, but it is some sort of object lesson in conservation.—F.E.A.*

The Big Thicket is full of things that do not follow designated patterns but take surprising turns. Sour Lake is an example. Located in Hardin County at the southern tip of the Thicket where the forest opens out on a small prairie, slightly higher than the forest land around it, Sour Lake overlooks the lake which gives it its name. Two seemingly inexhaustible natural resources—oil and health-giving mineral springs —have at times brought the town wide-spread fame and a temporary rise in population and income; yet, for one cause or another, the outside capital which was developing these resources has found greener fields and moved on, again leaving Sour Lake a quiet small town, supported chiefly by the agricultural areas that surround it.

The town owes its being and most constant fame to twenty-seven highly mineral springs, all with different therapeutic components, which overflow to form the lake that gives the town its name, although for many years it was known as Sour Springs.

Even the soil around the springs is highly mineral; and, while there are other areas of Texas which have mineral springs, Sour Lake stands out because of the variety of mineral elements found in its soil and water. In addition to the salt and petroleum common to coastal areas, these springs have a high content of calcium, magnesium, sodium, potassium, chlorine, carbohydrates, and sulphates.

Why this is true geologically is not definitely known, but at a meeting of the Texas Scientific and Historical Societies, held in the Big Thicket somewhere in the early 1930's on Pop Jackson's hunting reserve, there was much discussion of this matter. Some strong claims were made that many of the oddities of the Big Thicket resulted from the fact that, toward the end of the ice age, the melting glaciers in northern United States and southern Canada pushed land and water southward and at times to the sides— both east and west—in the Mississippi Valley, as silt was shoved away from the main stream of water flowing from the melting glaciers. This excess of water also caused high tides which swept back inland even after the marine age of the Texas coasts had passed. There was argument, of course, both for and against this theory.

Regardless of the cause, at some time in the fluctuating hot and cold ages of the world, nature washed up a nice mess of oil, minerals, and soil and left them in the little natural clearing around Sour

171

Lake. Not content, she built up underground pressures that pushed the mineral-laden springs to the surface.

As early as can be determined Indians knew of the existence of the sour springs. They also knew of their medicinal value, and had legends of the manner in which this knowledge came to them. Once such tale of Indian discovery of the springs is the legend of the white doe. My Grandmother Garrison was born near Woodville. Her father, Sam Belt, was agent and friend of the Alabamas, and Granny was steeped in Indian lore and tales of the Big Thicket. I have run across the "white doe" tale several times, not very well documented; but here it is, as Granny used to tell it.

One summer Indians living on the coast near what is now High Island were swept with a plague that threatened to wipe out the whole tribe. The medicine men were powerless before this great illness, and one day the chief's beloved daughter died. That night the girl appeared to her father in a dream and told him that she would come back to earth in another form and lead the tribe to a place of healing, and she promised that the plague would disappear if everyone would bathe in the magic water they would find there, and drink from the healing springs.

The next morning a beautiful white doe appeared before the chief's wigwam. In some mysterious way the doe made the chief understand that he and his people were to follow her. He agreed, and the doe started out, followed by a slow procession of sick and well. She led them to the edge of a great dark forest; then she plunged into the thick undergrowth. The Indians followed until she brought them to a halt on the banks of a beautiful small lake surrounded by a clearing and fed by many springs. For a moment she stood and looked into the chief's eyes, then she leaped into the forest and disappeared. As the chief's daughter had directed in the vision, the Indians drank the water from the springs and bathed in the lake, and soon they were well again.

Whether this legend was based on a general experience of wandering Indian tribes, we do not know, but we do find that the knowledge of the healing sour springs was common among Indian tribes from the Mexican border to the Louisiana line. The Tejas came often. The Karankawas came up from the coast. The Ais, and the savage tribes from the north came, and groups that were normally sworn enemies met at Sour Springs and bathed in and drank the healing waters. From father to son in the tribes came the knowledge of the whereabouts of the medicinal springs, and there was an unspoken agreement that this place was for all—a place of peace where a sacred truce was to be observed by those who came there seeking healing..

Legend also colors the story of the discovery of the springs by Stephen Jackson, the first white settler in Hardin County. Jackson came to Texas in 1835 and settled on the league of land which was granted him by the Mexican government. This grant included the tract from which bubbled the sour springs. Apparently Jackson did not explore all of his holdings when he first gained title to them. The story of the way Jackson discovered the springs is one told by the late Moscow Pevito, cattleman and rice farmer who settled just south of Nome in 1848. Pevito's story describes how Jackson and some of his hands had been riding the range all one hot summer day, rounding up broomtails for breaking. They were thirsty, and when they rode into a clearing and saw a nice clear lake, ponies and men made a dash for the water. After one sniff, the ponies threw up their heads and refused to drink, but Jackson dismounted, and, saying he was thirsty enough to drink anything, took a big swallow of water. One was enough. He leaped to his feet and yelled, "My God, boys! That water's poison. I'll die sure. Do something quick!"

But there was nothing to do, and Jackson didn't die. In fact, he soon felt better, and he was convinced that the water was medicinal. He spread the news of his discovery, and other people soon started coming to try the water out. Then someone decided that if drinking the water was good, bathing in it might double the benefit. They tried it and went away telling tales of miraculous cures for everything from eye trouble to gout and skin troubles.

Jackson built his home near the lake he had discovered, and the settlement which sprang up around Jackson's home became Sour Lake, the oldest community in Hardin County. This little settlement was in existence in 1837, for it appears on a map made by Stephen F. Austin and dated in that year.

In 1845 Sour Lake was a well-frequented health resort. The ailing came by covered wagon, train, horseback, carriage, and buggy. Some even walked. Later the Texas and New Orleans Railroad ran within seven miles of Sour Lake; it designated a stop as Sour Lake Station, and there was always a hack waiting at train time to carry visitors out to the springs. Some reports claim that people came to Sour Lake (or Sour Springs, as it was first called) from as far off as New York. This claim, however, may have been confused with visitors to Sour Lake during the oil boom.

Dr. Marant was the first to capitalize very much on the curative water. He used the name Sour Springs and advertised that the water would cure almost anything, but stress was laid on the benefits to those who suffered from skin disorders, digestive troubles, and muscular aches.

Visitors to Sour Lake Springs described the wells as having a great deal of sulphuric gas; and the taste of the water was said to have "a pleasant titillating sub-acid taste". The baths were called very exhilarating and invigorating in their effects.

Railroad service was discontinued during the Civil War, and the only use made of the tracks was as a trail for pedestrians and horseback riders through the swampy lowlands. By the end of the war tall saplings had grown up between the rails; nevertheless people still went to Sour Lake by "horsepower" or any other available transportation.

The customers must have been satisfied for there was a constant flow of visitors to the wells where pieces of pipe had been pushed two or three inches into the ground, and as the oil flowed up through these pipes, attendants handed out glasses of "water"— an oily fluid, which was probably almost pure crude oil. The customers paid twenty-five cents a glass for this potion, and natives of the area claim that this was probably the highest price that crude oil ever brought in its history.

In the early 1860's Sam Houston spent a month at Sour Springs. He was suffering from his old war wounds, and from a great

174

69. The Springs Hotel (Courtesy Clyde Gray's Heritage Garden, Woodville).

despondency over the Civil War and his unpopularity because of his stand against the secession of Texas from the Union. Houston does not seem to have benefited from his stay at the springs, for his former slave Jeff Hamilton wrote: "When he came back home, he was in worse shape than when he left."

Probably a major cause of Houston's lack of response to the cures was that while he was at the springs he received the news of the capture of Vicksburg by Grant on the 8th of July.

The springs continued to hold public interest, and *The Texas Almanac* of 1867, in describing Hardin County and its resources, says: "The celebrated Sour Lake Springs are in this county, and are much resorted to, but are destined to much greater reputation than they have ever yet obtained. They are, in many respects, the most remarkable springs known."

This prediction of such a rosy future was all the more remark-

175

able because at the time it was made Sour Lake had only ten voters: J. M. Carpenter, Horace and Reed Rogers, Nathan Jordan, Joseph Mobray and son Gus, Ambrose Merchant, Ambrose Jackson, O. Magnus, and Stephen Jackson, son of the founder of the settlement.

But even though the springs continued to be well known and much frequented, no one seems to have made much profit from them until the 1880's when the resort was bought by F. J. Willis of Galveston. Willis had the capital to improve the wells, and he built bath houses, and a luxurious two-story hotel in white-columned, deep-verandahed southern style. The Springs Hotel was well managed. There was good food, companionship for those who wanted to compare ailments and the progress of cures, and at night there was dancing for those who came with the social angle more in view. For the romantic there was a small summerhouselike pavilion in the lake. It was connected to the shore by an ornamental footbridge and served as a good place to end a stroll and watch the moon rise or listen to the music of a string band playing on the hotel verandah. Soon the resort attracted many wealthy and socially prominent people, and Sour Lake was frequently referred to as "The Saratoga of the South."

Oddly enough Sour Lake had a competitor only a few miles away. Here, too, there were mineral springs, some say seven; some say nine. This group of springs was discovered in the 1850's by J. F. Cotton. In 1879 P. S. Watts promoted the resort, which was called Saratoga after the New York spa. It boasted nothing so elaborate as the Springs Hotel, but it had cabins for rent, and a pavilion built over the wells where the customers could rest, visit, and drink the mineral waters. The discovery of oil in 1902 brought the Saratoga resort days to an end, and by 1948 only one spring was still in good condition.

Besides lacking the Springs Hotel and having fewer springs, Saratoga lacked Dr. Mud, a personage who, with a little more publicity, might well have developed into a sort of Paul Bunyan of the Big Thicket. There are several stories about the origin of Dr. Mud. One is that he had been a slave belonging to Joseph

70. Big Sandy Creek.

Pevito (brother of Moscow) who settled just south of Nome adjoining Moscow in 1848. This account said that Dr. Mud's real
name was Bazile, and that he was well known in the community
around the springs for his knowledge of the healing properties of
the water and the mud. He was a sort of medicine man for the

177

Negroes, and after he was freed he devoted his full time to his "practice." He moved to the springs and had "patients" among the whites as well as the Negroes.

Another version of Dr. Mud's background says that he belonged to one of the Cades at High Island where he was reared. This version says that he broke horses on the Cade ranch until he was crippled up so badly that he could no longer ride. Some time later he came to Sour Springs, and since there was no doctor there, and since he had an evident knowledge of how to use the waters and mud, he attached himself to the place as an attendant in the bath houses. His skill at massage and his effective use of mud packs soon gained him popularity and fame, and he was much in demand for his "cures."

The name "Dr. Mud" was given the Negro by J. Brooks Hamilton of Houston, a frequent visitor to the springs. It was Hamilton, too, who gave Dr. Mud the tall stiff white hat he always wore. This hat was one that was popular as a campaign hat worn during the presidential race when Grover Cleveland was running for President of the United States.

As his clients remember Dr. Mud, he was tall and thin, and had a straggling beard, and, in addition to the high hat, he always wore a long-tailed coat. His coat sleeves were too short, and his pants and coat did not meet, nor were the pants long enough. Newcomers found him very comical to look at.

Pranksters claimed all sorts of fake ailments, giving ridiculous names for them and asking Dr. Mud to prescribe for them. Without batting an eyelash, he unhesitatingly pointed out the type of mud packs or waters the patient needed, generally a combination from several wells, which he designated by numbers.

Dr. Mud knew where to look in the lake bottom for the mud for each type of treatment he used, and he knew how to make and apply packs for healing or beauty treatment. Many ladies visited Sour Lake and used the mud prescribed by Dr. Mud to improve their complexions. For the treatment he gave them mud that they put on at night and left on their faces until morning when it had dried into a sort of mask which they either washed or peeled off.

71. Climax hardwoods in Boggy Creek bottom.

He also had boxes of fine soil which he gave the ladies to use for face powder, probably something akin to the "prepared chalk" which was a popular face powder at the turn of the century.

Dr. Mud was a diplomat, too as evidenced in a story told by one of the "doctor's" regular patrons. One evening three rather homely women arrived at the Springs from New Orleans. After they were settled in their rooms, they walked over to see the lake and the wells. They saw Dr. Mud, and recognized him from the descriptions they had heard, so they went over and asked him to get them some beauty mud.

Dr. Mud looked at them, then said, "Yes, Ma'am, I will give you some nice beauty mud, but I don't think you needs it."

After the women left he commented that he didn't want to hurt their feelings, but that they were so ugly nothing could beautify them.

Early in the 1900's the Springs Hotel burned; much of the land around the wells had been bought or leased by the oil companies interested in the newly found oil strike. Dr. Mud died in 1903, and interest in Sour Lake as a health resort died.

As late as 1925 there was still an indoor swimming pool filled with tepid water that smelled strongly of its various mineral properties with sulphur predominant. The oil boom was over, and the town had dwindled away until it had none of its former glamor, but the swimming pool was popular with the younger set of the middle 'twenties, particularly those of Beaumont. It was a time before municipal, home, or club pools, and, roads being what they were then, going to the beach took time, planning, and courage. There was Lake Sabine at Port Arthur, but there again it took fortitude to brave the mosquitoes. Sour Lake offered a pleasant drive, possibly a roadside picnic, a swim, and all within a reasonable distance and space of time for an evening date.

There have been several attempts to rejuvenate Sour Lake as a resort—some within the past twenty years, but after a few publicity stories and stock-selling attempts, the efforts have "died a'borning."

The little town still has its sour springs, the medicinal muds are still available, but no Indians go there to bathe and have peaceful pow wows. The Springs Hotel, with its prominent guests, is only a memory, and Dr. Mud no longer lives to exercise his healing skill, except in the legends that are told about him.

# A FAMILY FULL OF LEGENDS

BY ELLEN WALKER RIENSTRA

*There's no need to go into Mrs. Rienstra's family background and her connection with the Big Thicket. She is the great-granddaughter of William Hooks and the granddaughter of Bud Hooks, two of the central characters in "A Family Full of Legends."—F.E.A.*

The Big Thicket attracted a strange type of people to its abundance of timber and game. It abounded with mosquitoes, poisonous snakes, wildcats, bears, and wolves, and the people who came there were of necessity the hardiest of their species, a fact which they and their descendants were very proud of. Since the density of the Thicket prevented much unnecessary travel, the earliest pioneers had to be content with solitude. In fact, the Thicket, to most of them, was a refuge in which they could live their own particular lives as they wanted. To this day most of them still feel the same way.

From the time that the first settlers penetrated its outer barriers until the present day, the Big Thicket exercised its influence on its people until gradually a unique way of life was formed. The people of the Thicket country evolved their own customs, manner of

181

72. Ellen Walker Rienstra.

speech, and way of life. Such a land is invariably the mother of
legends, and present-day members of old Thicket families treasure
tales of the exploits of their own particular ancestors. The Hooks
family typifies this process.

In 1849, William Hooks and his wife, Martha, made their way
in a covered wagon from Early County, Georgia, to East Texas.
There were several reasons for their coming. There was at this
time in the country a general fever to move westward, and William's brother Augustus Hooks was married to a girl who had folks
in Thicket country. Through them, tales of the good living to be
made there had reached Georgia. Also, William's wife and her
sister, Sarah, married to William's brother Allen, had some family
in Georgia, mostly their stepmother, that they were just as glad to
be leaving.

At any rate, William and Martha, called "Pap" and "Ma" by
their twelve children, came to Texas and first settled across from
Weiss Bluff on Belreaux Slough. After their son Tom. almost

73. William Hooks (Pap) (Courtesy Dr.
Allen Hooks).

drowned in the river, they moved briefly to Spurger, and then to
a farm slightly south of Kountze, where the majority of their children were born. They are buried near this farm.

Pap was a physically small man, standing about 5′ 8″ in his
bare feet. He had a short, full beard and a thick head of hair,
which he kept all his life. His daughter Dode said she only saw
him clean-shaven one time, and she didn't like it at all. Old John
Sims, who used to pass Pap's house carrying freight to Town Bluff,
used to say that he could remember Pap standing out by a stump
in his front yard, looking like a "big hairy animal" reading the
*Galveston News.*

He was a shrewd man, and, after some years of raising cotton
and sugar cane for syrup, was somewhat better off money-wise
than his neighbors. He kept his money in his loft, and when he
needed any of it, he would send his boys after it. The story goes
that Pap and a Mr. Holland were the ones who determined the
sheriff of Hardin County; the sheriff had to put up a certain

amount of bond to run for office, and Pap and Mr. Holland were the only ones who could afford to put it up.

Like all his family, Pap had a great affection for his kinfolk, and would immediately jump to their defense on any matter, regardless of how small. However, he wasn't much for visiting. His brother Jim, of whom Pap was very fond, lived in Spurger. He hadn't seen him in ten years. At one time he had business in Spurger, and after he had finished it, he started toward home with the intention of stopping in to see his brother, whose house was on the way. Just on the other side of his brother's house, he met a man on a mule who he knew was a local fellow. He stopped him and asked him if he knew his brother Jim. The man said he did. Pap asked him how his brother was doing, and the man said that he was doing just fine. Since he knew that his brother was well and didn't need anything, Pap passed by his brother's house and went back to his own farm.

Pap's daughter Dode was married to a schoolteacher, a Mr. Leving G. Roberts. They were having marital difficulties, and Dode had come to Pap's house to live. One day Lev came to the house with the idea of patching up the fuss. Pap was in the field plowing in his shirttail. Ma, being a neat sort of person, sent pants out to the field by one of the boys. She thought that Lev, being a schoolteacher, might be a little easier to shock than the ordinary person, and that Pap should wear pants while he visited with him. Lev and Dode were making up their quarrel when Pap came in from the field at noon, whistling. His pants were folded over his arm. He threw them across the bed and sat down to visit.

Pap's brother Augustus Hooks was a strange gentleman, some of whose children were also rather unusual. When Pap came to Texas in 1849, Aus came too, with a wagon and two oxen. As he was crossing a river, one of his oxen died. He was so infuriated that he killed his other ox, burned his wagon, and walked back to Georgia. The next year he tried again and, meeting no major calamity on the way nor causing one himself, made it to the Texas Thicket country and settled down permanently. He was exactly the opposite from Pap in that he showed a tendency to be extremely particular about everything. In fact, he had been known to pick the splinters off his rail fence so that it would look neater.

One of Aus's sons, May Hooks, loved to fight (someone said he'd have to fight with a name like that). He and Warren Collins, one of the toughest fighting men in the Thicket, fought every Saturday at Old Hardin, where a group of men would gather to play Bull Pen. There actually wasn't supposed to be any fighting at these gatherings, but somehow it always turned out that way. Bull Pen is a game in which everyone gets in a circle, with one person in the middle. The person in the middle tries to hit someone in the outside circle with a ball, without that person's catching the ball. If the person in the middle hits someone, they have to exchange places, putting the person who was hit in the middle. In this instance, May Hooks was the man in the middle, trying to hit someone in the circle with the ball. Warren Collins got down and began pawing the ground and bellowing like a bull. Collins was bald-headed, and May threw the ball and hit him right on top of his head. Warren came toward him, and they met right at the edge of the ring, fighting like wildcats. Warren Collins won that fight; the only man in the Thicket who could get the best of Collins physically was a blacksmith, whose name, unfortunately, has been lost to posterity.

Perhaps the most famous of all Aus's offspring is the redoubtable Gus Hooks, whose chief claim to fame is that he was the swiftest runner anywhere around. He is credited with having run a race against a man on a horse and won. A bootlegger of some renown, Gus had two houses, just around a bend in the road from each other, and two wives. The story goes that when one of Gus's sons was convicted of robbery and sent to the penitentiary, Gus was present at the trial. After the sentence had been pronounced, Gus went up to Judge L. B. Hightower and told him, "Judge, there ain't no use to send that boy up there. He won't be satisfied." He wasn't. He escaped two or three times, always coming back to East Texas. Authorities would catch him and take him back, but he would always manage to get away again.

Many East Texas people came from states in the Old South, as

74. Lum (Courtesy Dr. Allen Hooks).    75. Day (Courtesy Dr. Allen Hooks

had Pap. Consequently, feeling ran high in sympathy with the South when the war between the States began. Pap's wild son Day was one of the first to join.

Day's older brother Lum was the oldest of Pap's twelve and as quiet and steady a boy as Day was wild. He succeeded his father as county commissioner while he was still too young to vote, having gotten all the education that was available to him, and had the promise of a good career ahead of him. However, when Day joined the Confederate Army, Lum did too, but the only reason he did was to keep Day out of trouble. Major Dark, a friend of the Hooks family, used his influence to have Lum immediately transferred to Galveston so he would be safely away from any fighting. Ironically, he contracted typhus there and was sent home, where he died shortly thereafter.

Day went on in Gregg's Seventh Infantry Division to Vicksburg, where he and Zack Guynes, another Hardin County man, were captured, probably somewhere around Fort Donelson. They were held by the Yankees until winter. That winter, it turned bitter cold, and Day's feet froze so badly that he could not walk. Zack either had to carry him or leave him to die, so he carried him on his back through the snow. Whether they escaped, were exchanged, or paroled is not known, but they somehow got to Virginia, where Day worked as a payroll wagon driver for Lee's Army of Northern Virginia, because he couldn't walk.

When the war ended, he, Zack Guynes, and two other men that were with them each determined to steal themselves a Yankee horse to ride home on, but Day was the only one who succeeded. The men took turns riding the one horse home.

Day and the other men returned to Hardin County war heroes. Day's toes were so badly frostbitten that he lost all but five of them, but he said often that he hoped and prayed that someday he would have a chance to crawl on his hands and knees through the snow to do something for Zack Guynes. The war was a horror to him, and in later years he refused to talk about it. The loss of his much-loved older brother, Lum, was hard for Day to bear, and the knowledge that Lum had joined simply to keep him out of trouble probably made the cup more bitter. It was a much sadder and wiser Day who named his oldest son William Columbus Hooks, called Lum.

Pap's next son, Buck, was different from his two older brothers entirely. He hated to work, and seems to have been something of a dandy. A tale is told of his oldest son, Charlie Hooks, when he was in Houston for awhile. He fell in love with a lady there and got into some sort of trouble because of it, and he gave her one of his father's best horses, which he had with him at the time. Buck was perturbed at the loss of his horse, and went to Houston with the idea of getting it back. When he met the lady he was so charmed by her that he left the horse with her. When he got home, he declared that she was so lovely that if he had had another horse, he would have given it to her, too.

Perhaps the best-known of Pap's children were his two youngest sons, Ben and Bud, bear hunters of the Big Thicket. Ben, the older of the two, was a slender man, lithe as a greyhound, with chiseled features and high cheekbones. He had an ability to make

76. Buck (Courtesy Dr. Allen Hooks).    77. Ben (Courtesy Dr. Allen Hooks).

and invest money and a love of machinery of any type, traits which were to serve him well in his later ventures.

Silent to the point of being taciturn at times, he nevertheless was loyal to his friends and extremely generous to them. Ben carried his loyalty to his friends to a great degree. It had to be proved to him plainly that one of his friends was double-crossing him, or he wouldn't believe anything that anyone told him about them. He had a short, unfortunate romance with a young lady with whom he was very much in love—probably the grand passion of his life. The young lady seemed to return his affections, and they planned to be married very shortly. Ben's brother Sam told Ben that she was rather free with her affections; however, Ben refused to believe him. Sam bet Ben that he could date her himself, which he did. Ben severed relations with the young lady after that, later marrying Zuleika Robertson of Batson, a young lady "without flaw," and breaking at least one other hopeful heart in the process, who, according to her family, "walked the floor and wrung her hands" the night he was married.

Pap was dead by this time, and Ben and Bud had built for their mother a house on a little knoll in Kountze on which Pap had wanted to live (Bud lived with Ma as long as she lived, then stayed on in the house with his own wife after she died). Ben, as did Bud, had decided early in life that farming was not for him, and he made his living in various ways. He ran a store in Kountze and at one time owned several saloons. In 1904 he ventured into oil, perhaps the most monetarily fortunate move of his life. He brought in the Saratoga Oil Field. Using small hand pumps— "strong-armed johnnies"—and a bolted-together derrick (Carter Hart says you could roll it around on the ground without its coming apart), Ben and a group of his friends and brothers brought in the well which was the first of the great field. Ben personally oversaw the whole operation, staying at the well day and night, and putting his mechanical ingenuity to work on various problems that occurred with the drilling process. He said later that he reckoned he was the first man to put a strainer on the bottom of an oil pipe to make it produce.

Ben and Sam, the thrifty ones, put up most of the money to drill the well, and they staked their brothers George and Paul to a share in it. When the well came in, all of them had more than enough money with which to do what they wanted. Ben and Sam saved and invested theirs, but Bud and George spent theirs quickly.

Around 1902, during the height of the Spindletop Oil Boom, Ben and Jack Dies, his sometime partner, were staying at a hotel in Sour Lake. Dies had a tendency to wander around in his sleep. In the middle of the night, Ben woke up and missed him, and when he started looking for him, heard a commotion going on at the front door. When he went to see what it was, he found Dies hollering and cussing and raising cain and pounding on the front door. He took Dies back upstairs with him, but by the time he got him upstairs, everyone in the hotel knew about it. Ben was an habitually late sleeper, and he came down to breakfast the next morning long after everyone else was already down. They had been talking about the commotion the night before, and Dies

189

had told everyone that it was Ben that had been raising the cain. He told them, "Now, that Hooks fellow is all right; he'll be fine when he gets up." Ben came down knowing nothing about it, and he said later that he wondered why everyone was cutting their eyes around at him and looking at him sideways. He didn't know what was the matter until Jack told him. Ben said he ought to 've beat him to death right there.

There is another story that has to do with Jack Dies and a Negro porter, Jonah Arline. The Arlines were a well-to-do white family who owned slaves before the War, and from their slaves emerged a large Negro family, also named Arline, who played a great part in Thicket history. Several of the Arline boys were porters at the saloon that was owned by Ben and later by Jack Dies. Every night after work, Jonah would take a little bottle of whisky with him and, smoking his pipe, ride his old gray horse to his home north of Hardin. After he died, people soon began to say that he had made that trip so much in his lifetime that he still made it after he was dead. Jack Dies, on an early morning trip past the Negro cemetery where Jonah was buried, saw a man on a gray horse, smoking a pipe, coming toward him. It almost scared Dies to death. He said later that if he hadn't had Little Son (one of Negro twins, Little Son and Big Son Fields) with him, he'd have turned back. The "ghost" turned out to be simply a traveler on a gray horse, who happened to be smoking a pipe at the time.

Bud, the youngest member of the family, who was so spindly and small when he was a boy that his mother made him chew tobacco as a cure for worms, grew up to be the biggest and best looking of the Hooks men. He stood almost six feet barefooted, (and he often went barefooted), and he had the broad-shouldered, narrow-hipped build of a good athlete. He had a big head of iron-gray hair (white in his later years) which required a size 7⅞ hat, which he had to specially order. His skin was swarthy and his eyes were blue. He cared nothing for his personal appearance and thought nothing of going anywhere in work clothes. Although he had an ability to make money and often had plenty, the only importance he attached to it was what it could buy him. He especi-

78. Bud (Courtesy Dr. Allen Hooks).

ally liked good watches, fine dogs, and guns, and it was said that it you saw a man in khakis and a jumper but with a fine watch, a $150 gun and at least one good hound, that man was Bud Hooks.

Bud loved to  go barefoot (or else just hated to wear shoes). He was probably barefooted at some of the most important moments of his life. When his son was born, after a long labor and a difficult birth, he went to town to get some medicine. He had been barefooted, so he simply stayed that way. He never walked fast; when he was in a hurry, he trotted. He was trotting barefooted into town when he passed Buck's stepson, Jim Allums, sitting on his front porch. He yelled happily, "Hey, Jim, I've got me a boy as big as a skinned mule."

Naturally enough, Bud wasn't too careful about shaving every day, and his beard happened to grow naturally into an approximation of a Van Dyke. One day in town he was sitting on a bench next to a man who had a long, pointed nose and a chin that almost came up to meet it. Somebody saw them sitting side by side, and exclaimed, "Well, there sits the Devil and Jesus Christ!"

Wherever he was, Bud was the center of any crowd because of his sense of humor. He was the wit of any camp, and never seemed to be without a reply to a situation. He loved animals of any kind, and after oil brought the money, he surrounded his house with pens of animals, wild and tame, including deer and bear. He bought an elk at one time, and some of the Negroes were helping him unload it. After the elk was in its pen and they had finished the job, he said, "Well, boys, I sure do appreciate this. If any of you ever have an elk to unload, just let me know and I'll be glad to help you unload it."

Mr. Ed Gross, former mayor of Beaumont, was riding in the woods with his wife one day and came upon Bud sitting in the woods with his truck and dogs. He seldom hunted alone, but this particular time he probably just wanted to get out in the woods by himself. Mr. Gross asked him, "Are you in trouble?"

Bud said, "I don't think I am. The grand jury's not in session and I don't think my wife's mad at me."

Killraine, a Negro who was quite a colorful fellow in his own right (he was supposed to have been the only Negro to be allowed in Saratoga, sundown or not), worked off and on for Bud throughout the years. He cooked for the bear hunts, and hunted cattle in the woods several times with Bud. One time, they, Leake Bevil, and Bud's daughter Allie were cattle-hunting toward Nona, catching cattle and branding them as they went. They were approaching a small branch with bushes hiding it. A little wild pig ran out of the bushes under Bud's horse's feet. The horse threw him, and the fall injured his back. He was unable to move, and while his daughter Allie rushed home to get a car, Killraine picked him up and put him on his back. He carried him to the place where Allie brought the car—which was quite a distance. Bud was in awful pain at the moment, and was incapacitated for a long time after the accident, but the only thing he said about any of it was, "Kil, you sure make a good saddle hoss."

People had many reasons for liking Bud Hooks, but perhaps

the strangest reason ever voiced was that of old Dan Brown, who thought Bud was such a good fighter and so physically strong that he wanted to give him one of his daughters. Bud gracefully declined.

The same Dan Brown had several sons, one of whom was named Van, who was a little "tetched in the head." Van was in the woods one day, and his brother Bob saw him and remarked to their father that Van was down in the woods. Old Dan said, "Bob, take your Winchester down there; you might get a pop at him."

By 1906 Bud and Ben had established their reputations as hunters of the Louisiana black bear that inhabited the Thicket at that time (the Saratoga Oil Field had by that time afforded both men the money and leisure to do all the hunting they wanted to). They had a bear camp in the Thicket, named Hooks Lodge, and would take large parties of hunters into the Thicket to hunt with them.

They owned eight of the finest bear hounds in the county; an incomparable pack. The names of the dogs were Ramsey, Buck, Ring, Drag, Alex, Big Foot, Jack, and the legendary bear hound Dandy, the start dog, the most important dog in the pack. He was the most valuable bear hound that any of them ever had. He was a big dog, a thoroughbred redbone hound that had been trained to run panther; Bud got him at some kennels in West Texas. He ran the first bear trail he ever found, and ran them the rest of his life. His chief virtues were that he would run only a bear trail, and that he could smell a trail so cold that no other dog could smell it. Dandy was far too valuable to risk fighting with the bears, and as he got older, the hunters increasingly coddled him by letting him work up a cold trail and then pulling him out when the trail was hot enough for the other dogs to smell. He became deaf in his old age and moved increasingly slower as the years went by, but he remained the best bear dog in the Thicket. No dog ever topped him.

Carter Hart is the only man left alive who used to hunt with Bud and Ben. He says that they would go out the evening before a bear hunt, with groceries, dog feed, and horse feed all loaded in a wagon, with, of course, saddle horses and the bear pack. The next morning, they would saddle the horses and neck up the dogs, two by two. The only dog that was not necked up was Dandy. The hunters would then mount up and start to move toward bear country. Dandy would work up the trail. When Dandy would jump (when the trail got hot and he began going faster), they turned some of the other dogs loose (usually Alex and Ramsey). The dogs would be whining at their heels, eager to be let loose, but they would never bark. Then in just a little while, the hunters turned the whole pack loose. "They would go just as straight to old Dandy as you could shoot a gun." Then the hunters would choose their individual ways to go, according to which way they thought the bear was going. Bears usually ended up in or somewhere near the Hurricane, a patch of Thicket where a tornado had destroyed all the big timber and the brush had grown up twice as thick as the rest of it.

Whoever found the bear first had the shot at it, then he signalled the others by three blasts on the cow horn that all of them carried. The dead bear was taken back to camp, where it was then skinned and cleaned amidst much laughing, joking, and telling of tales.

Perhaps the most spectacular incident in the lives of Ben and Bud is what became known later as the Woodville Shooting Scrape. Hardin County politics often got down to brass tacks, and feeling always ran high around election time. Feeling was especially bitter about the sheriff's race in which Lev Roberts, the Hooks boys' brother-in-law, defeated Bill Lyons, the incumbent sheriff. Several fights resulted, one of which was in a saloon, between Lewis Ferguson (for Roberts), and one of the Humble boys (for Lyons). After the fight, as Ferguson was walking home along the railroad track with his dog, one or both of the Humble boys, Sam and Pleas, shot and killed him. Sam and Pleas disappeared.

The boys' father, old Jim Humble, a good man, seemed to want to find the boys, but they didn't turn up for awhile. Bud, one of Roberts' deputies, was at the Kountze Courthouse window not long after that, and saw Sam and Pleas go into the woods toward

Cypress Creek. Bud followed them at a distance into the woods, staying hidden. He heard them give some whistles and figured that they were meeting someone, but he came upon them in a clearing too suddenly to hide himself. Sam and Pleas were there, and the old man, and the youngest brother, Billy. All of the men were armed. Billy had a shotgun in his hands and seemed extremely nervous. Afraid of what he would do with it, Bud said later that he had never been so eloquent in his life. He started off with "Well, Jim, I see you've found them," and continued in the same vein. They must have been dumfounded at his being there, because they went quietly with him to jail.

When Sam and Pleas were brought to trial, feeling was so high in Hardin County that the venue was changed to Tyler County. The case was tried, and the jury acquitted Pleas Humble. Sam Humble was convicted of manslaughter and sentenced to five years in prison; however, the district attorney, suspecting that the Humbles had a strong partisan on the jury, deliberately made a reversible error. In his jury argument, he pointed to Sam and said, "There he sits silent in the face of this damning testimony!" Sam was granted a new trial, because an attorney's comment on the defendant's refusal to testify is an automatic reversible error.

It was to the second trial, on June 8, 1896, in the Woodville Courthouse, that people flocked, including men who avidly supported both sides of the affair. Bud and Ben, in addition to being Lev's brothers-in-law, were uncles-in-law of Lewis Ferguson, the slain man. Besides, Bud was deputy sheriff. They went to Woodville as Ferguson supporters. Among these men were Ped Ferguson, Lewis' brother, and Hardee Turner, brother of Lewis' wife. Both sides suspected there would be shooting, so all men came armed. Ped Ferguson stationed his brother across the street with several Winchesters, with orders to pass them out if necessary. The trial went on until noon, when it was adjourned for dinner and everyone filed downstairs.

Ped Ferguson, rather hot-headed and hopping for revenge, exchanged words on the way down with old Jim Humble. Ped tried to get his gun out. Hardee Turner, a quiet sort, tried to calm Ped down, but Ben, just behind them, said to Hardee, "For God's sake, let him alone!"

When the crowd broke out onto the street, the shooting started. Bud and Ped Ferguson were shooting at old Jim, who, unafraid, was walking steadily toward them, firing his gun. Bud said later that the barrel of his gun looked six inches around. When old Jim's gun clicked on an empty chamber, he yelled at Bud, "Go ahead and shoot, goddam you, I'm out of ca'tridges."

Bud said, "Oh, well, if you're out of ca'tridges, I'll go shoot at somebody else."

One of the Humble boys was shooting from behind a tree; a nonpartisan bystander was so incensed at his hiding that he put a gun to Humble's ribs and made him move from behind the tree. Ben, a little behind Bud and Ped, noticed gunfire coming from the direction of the Courthouse. He looked closer and saw that it was coming from a side window. He went around to the back, went in, and discovered Billy Humble firing at Bud and Ped from the window. Ben said later that, in the split-second before he shot Billy, when Billy turned and saw him, he almost looked ashamed of himself for firing from cover, and he appeared to try to hide his gun. Ben put his gun to Billy's stomach and fired.

As Bud and Ben both said later, although there were more than thirty shots fired, everyone shot too fast to do much damage, and there were not many injuries. Billy Humble, shot by Ben, was the most serious one; it was generally believed that he would die. Old Jim Humble had numerous flesh wounds, Pleas Humble suffered a slight wound in the leg, and Bud had bullet holes in his coat and hat.

After their ammunition was gone, Sam and Pleas Humble, Clint Whittington and Bill Lyons ran (one member of the group was said to have "vaulted a high board fence and left on a dead run"), but old Jim walked away. The Ferguson partisans called for their stashed Winchesters, but by this time, the Tyler County sheriff and Judge Nix came out to try to disarm everyone. Bud, however, wouldn't give up his Winchester, because he was afraid that the missing members of the Humble crowd might be hiding in buildings for the purpose of sniping at them. He raised his arms and held his Winchester above his head. Judge Nix came up and said in a stern voice, "Give me that gun!" thereby gaining for himself a reputation for bravery.

Bud wouldn't lower his gun, so the sheriff and half a dozen others reached for it and tried to pull it down. The gun didn't budge. Bud probably would have held it up until they thought of jerking his feet out from under him, but about this time Sheriff Roberts, who had been up in the courtroom talking to a witness and had come down as soon as possible, came up to the group and said, "Give them the gun, Bud. It's all right." Bud gave them the gun, but he, Ben, and Ped were put under arrest and their bond fixed at $300 each, "which they readily paid." Charges were later dropped against them.

Billy Humble survived his wound; Ben's bullet had hit a rib. Carter Hart tells of the time, years later, when he, Bud, and Carl Richardson were camped by the side of a road. Bud was lying on a cot, and the others were lounging around the camp. A man passed on the road. Bud said nothing for a minute, then asked Carter, "Carter, do you know who that was that passed here a minute ago?"

Carter said, "Yep."

"Who was it?"

"Billy Humble."

This was the first time that Bud had seen him since the shooting. In about thirty minutes, they saw Humble walking back (it is rumored that at this point one of the hunters exclaimed, "Here comes Humble with a Winchester, and we don't even have a pine knot"). Bud got up, walked out to the road, and said, "Hello Billy."

Humble said, "Howdy Bud." They shook hands. They talked a while, and Billy started on; Bud asked him to come back and go hunting with them that night. He said he might do it; however, as it turned out, he wasn't able to make it.

As Bud and Ben grew old in Kountze, living out their full lives,

197

the number of Hooks and stories increased yearly. The progeny of old William Hooks and his brothers and sisters spread so far throughout East Texas that in 1951 the General Crude Oil Company, which had oil interests in the area, insisted that a complete affidavit on Hooks and his family be prepared, because any transaction with any of the people in that area involved his descendants in some degree. This affidavit was signed by the last of his children to survive, his tenth child, George Washington Hooks.

# BIG THICKET BALLADRY

BY WILLIAM A. OWENS

*No one has collected more Big Thicket songs or studied them
more thoroughly than has Bill Owens. He was making the rounds
with a recording machine when both collectors and recording
machines were considered rarities. He cut the songs on aluminum
disks that had to be played with a cactus needle, and his record
of Ben Hooks' "Cattle in the Canebrake," made in 1938, still has
the fidelity given by most modern tape recorders.*

*Bill was East Texas from the start, having been born and raised
in the community of Pin Hook in Lamar County, and began
studying East Texas folk music seriously when he was doing his
master's work at Southern Methodist University. His first book,
SWING AND TURN: TEXAS PLAY-PARTY GAMES (1936) was an out-
growth of his thesis. In 1950 he published TEXAS FOLK SONGS
through the Texas Folklore Society. Most of the songs in this
book were collected in East Texas and the Thicket area. A lot of
folks in the Big Thicket still remember that Frank Dobie came
through on the trail of the Ben Lilly legend and that Bill Owens
was around hunting for the old songs.—F.E.A.*

The Big Thicket is both a fact and a fantasy, with
no definable overlapping of the two, geographi-
cally or otherwise, for the boundaries, like heat waves, shift with

79. William A. Owens.

the viewer. Nearly any Texan will say the Big Thicket is down in the southeast part, somewhere close to Louisiana. No one, Texan or not, can tell exactly where it begins or ends, or how to trace its lines north, south, east, west. For thirty years now, off and on, I have traveled up and down East Texas in search of the Big Thicket in any form. In Livingston they said, "Go down yan way a piece'n you'll come to it." At Liberty they said, "It's over yander where it's nothing but pineys a-living." At Fred, they thought it might be down among the swampers. I found a settlement called "Thicket" on the map and went to it. Even there, the storekeeper was somewhat unwilling to admit that he was in the "Big" Thicket, an unwillingness that I believe comes from the force and character of the place.

Early settlers pushing westward across the Sabine River encountered a vast region where heavy stands of longleaf yellow pine covered the sandy hillsides, where impenetrable thickets grew along the innumerable streams, where swamps big enough to be called swamps, or small enough to be called baygalls, grew thick with canebrakes and palmettos. No wonder they called it the *Big* Thicket. At first, they thought it covered all the area between the Old San Antonio Road, the *Camino Real,* and the coastal prairie, and reached from the Sabine River to the Brazos. Before long, they realized that the Trinity River formed the western boundary. Even so, the region was large. The *Camino Real* crossed the Sabine at Gaines Ferry, near San Augustine, and followed a general southwesterly course until it formed the north boundary of what is now Brazos County. The southern edge of that early Big Thicket followed the coastal prairie near Beaumont to Liberty on the Trinity.

In 1900, according to *The Texas Handbook,* the Big Thicket included all of part of the following counties: Hardin, Polk, Tyler, Jasper, Newton, Sabine, San Augustine, Angelina, Trinity, Montgomery, and Liberty. 1900 is a significant date. By then the pine forests were being cut away for lumber. In 1900, with the discovery of oil at Spindeltop, oil diviners and other explorers began to push deeper and deeper into the thickets.

In 1966 the pines have been mostly cut away, and the hardwoods are going fast. State and national highways through the area bear a heavy traffic of people who have never heard of the Big Thicket. Change is apparent, but not everywhere. There are still pockets of untouched land, settlements of old-time people, but in another generation they, too, will be gone.

In the beginning the Big Thicket was bounded on the east by the Neutral Ground, a fact that has added greatly to the fantasy. After the Louisiana Purchase, the United States and Spain were unable to agree on a boundary between Louisiana and Texas. In 1806 they agreed that the disputed area between the Arroyo Hondo on the east and the Sabine River on the west would be a Neutral Ground, with no settlers to be allowed. It became a refuge for outlaws, horse thieves, and gamblers, so lawless that military expeditions had to be mounted against them in the period from 1810 to 1812. When the United States acquired ownership in 1821 the area was cleared, but the bad reputation was already established. Some of those driven out crossed the Sabine into the Big Thicket, giving it for many the same bad reputation. Such a reputation hangs on.

"They's a heap o' bad blood in there that ain't never been bred out," I was told by an old man near Fred.

There were the lawless among early settlers in the Big Thicket. The majority, however, were in the main stream of western migration. Most of the people I interviewed when I was collecting songs there in 1937-1941 and 1952-1953 were born in the Big Thicket. Their parents, however, were more likely to have been born "back in the old country"—meaning Alabama, Mississippi, Tennessee, or some other Southern state.

The great number of early settlers in East Texas, as Barnes F. Lathrop has shown in his *Migration into East Texas, 1835-1860*, were descended from people who at the end of the Revolutionary War lived in the piedmont of Virginia and the Carolinas. From there they can be traced back to the English, Scotch, Irish, and Welsh settlers who first took up residence on the wilderness shore. They were not so much the well-to-do, who were able to establish and maintain plantations with the help of Negro slaves, but the poorer whites, who moved on to claim land of their own.

The Revolution over, the new territories opened to the west, and people, mostly young people, flowed out to claim the land. The movements of these people, their children, and their grandchildren, though fluid and overlapping, may be separated, as Lathrop shows, into three main streams. The upper stream, primarily from Virginia, secondarily from North Carolina and Maryland, went first to Kentucky and Ohio and became Texas settlers from Kentucky, Missouri, Indiana, and Illinois. A middle stream from North Carolina with a large tributary from Virginia and a smaller one from South Carolina flowed into Tennessee and on into Missouri and Arkansas. A lower stream, originating in Virginia but enlarged by settlers from North and South Carolina, flowed into Georgia and then on to Alabama, Mississippi, Arkansas, and Louisiana. This lower stream was the main one in the settlement of East Texas. The middle stream furnished about a third, the upper one no more than a tenth. The number of foreign born who arrived before 1860 is negligible.

The pattern of migration was remarkably uniform: young people went went far enough to take up new land, clear it, and wear it out. Most of them lived out their lives on this land. It was their children who moved on, to clear more land, live on it, and wear it out. On they went, crossing ridges, following valleys, looking for new places to live, new places not too different from the ones left behind. In wagons, in ox carts, on horseback, on foot they went, carrying little, for they had little to carry. They found the Big Thicket enough like the land they had left behind to feel at home. A little boy said to his father, "You'd think it was Arkansas if you didn't know it was Texas." Camping out under trees while they worked, they built log houses, covered them with hand-split boards, and chinked and daubed them with red clay. They built stick-and-dirt chimneys. Fireplaces were for heat and cooking, and for light at night, the only light they had except for the red smoky glare of a lightwood knot. They cleared only as much land as they could work with one horse hooked to a Georgia stock or kelly turning plow, enough land for a little cotton, a little corn—for a patch of sweet potatoes and black-eyed peas. Their cattle grazed on the open range. So did the razorback hogs. There was elbow room and to spare. They had no wish to obliterate the wilderness.

In 1850 the white population in nineteen East Texas counties was thirteen thousand plus; in 1860 it had jumped to eighty-seven thousand. During the war years, migration increased considerably, some say with the wrong kind of people: the deserters, jail breakers, men in any kind of trouble. GTT—"Gone to Texas"—was used in the old states to designate the ones who left for cause. GTT in the Big Thicket began to mean bad blood coming in. Bad blood or not, the people in East Texas had long been accustomed to horror, terror, death. On a succession of frontiers they had known enough of violence to expect it as a way of life.

There are ways to suggest the character of these people, but not to define it. They are too complex for easy definition. English, Scotch, Irish, Welsh in the beginning, by the time they reached the

80.  East Texas folk musicians.

Big Thicket the various strains had intermingled and become indistinguishable one from the other. Their names suggest national origins; their appearances do not. In appearance, the people ran to the gaunt—they called it "ga'nt"—in frame; in complexion to a sandy shade, often lost in the sallowness of malaria.

In religion, they were Baptists, Methodists, and Presbyterians by name, by belief strongly Calvinistic. "What is to be will be" was a faith to live by in the presence of death or disaster. The moral beliefs they held came mainly from their religion, from the Ten Commandments, learned by heart in childhood, brought to memory again by sermons under brush arbors.

In education Big Thicket people remained far behind. The schools they set up, like the schools on all the frontiers they had passed through, lasted only a few months a year and rarely got beyond reading, writing, and arithmetic. The ones who went to school were lucky if they learned to read and write. The others simply remained illiterate. No wonder outsiders thought the people "quare." Their language, brought to America in the late seventeenth and early eighteenth century, remained an oral language, uninfluenced by books other than the Bible. They "jined" the church and knew the best part of a pig is the "tenderline." To them a diaper was a hippen, a bull a hemin or a surly.

Through isolation, they preserved a language. Through isolation, they also preserved a folklore, especially in their ballads and songs. This brings us to the topic of this article.

Songs I have collected in the Big Thicket fall into three general types: ballads handed down from early English, Scotch, and Irish settlers; American imitations of these ballads; and comic songs, both imported and domestic. For this article I am omitting the religious songs—the white spirituals, the Sacred Harp songs, and the singing-school songs—all in a sense a part of the oral tradition but also preserved in printed versions sometimes available to the singers.

The ballads and songs say a great deal about the character of people in the Big Thicket. What made them cry? What made them laugh? Each is a special key to understanding. It is true that the same keys might be applied to people anywhere along the routes of migration through the Southern states.

The Big Thicket singer may call a ballad an "old fool song" and appear not to be touched by the story it tells. Underneath, he may be greatly affected, though he reveals his feelings only by the tempo and the timbre of his voice. In some cases, he may be openly emotional. On one occasion a gray-haired man leaned against the paling fence around his front yard and sang for me "Barbara Allen." When he came to the line "Young man I think you're dying" he let tears stand on his cheeks a moment and then brushed them away.

In a land where the swiftest punishment was a noose over the nearest limb, a ballad like "The Hangman's Rope" had a special meaning. Once in a recording session an old woman was singing this song for me. She sang the stanza:

> Oh, hangman, hangman, slack your rope
> And slack it for awhile,
> For I think I see my own dear father
> Come riding many a mile.

Then there was the question:

> Oh, father, did you bring me gold,
> And did you pay my fee,
> Or did you come to see me hanged
> On yander's gallows tree.

The answer of the father brought sadness to the faces.

> Oh, no, I did not bring you gold
> Nor did I pay your fee,
> And I have come to see you hanged
> On yander's gallows tree.

"He oughtn't to a done her thataway," another old woman whispered. She spoke the feelings of the singer and the listeners around her. Not till the sweetheart arrived with gold and freed the heroine did the sadness pass.

The effect of unrequited love is a recurring theme in the Brit-

ish ballads. It is also imitated in American ballads, as this version
of "The Tavern in the Town" shows:

> He went upstairs, the door he broke,
> And found her hanging by a rope;
> He took his knife and cut her down,
> And on her bosom these words he found:
> "Must I go bound and he go free,
> Must I love a man who don't love me?
> Oh, I have played the maiden's part
> And died for a man who broke my heart."

The people could also weep over men who had been part of the
American scene. Jesse James was a desperado; he was also a kind
of Robin Hood who robbed the rich and gave to the poor. His murder is the burden of an oft-sung refrain:

> Poor Jesse had a wife to mourn him all her life,
> His children they were brave,
> But the dirty little coward went and shot Mister Howard
> And they laid Poor Jesse in his grave.

But the man did not have to be a hero to make them cry, as this refrain shows:

> Oh, my name is Charles Guiteau,
> My name I'll never deny;
> For the murder of James A. Garfield
> I am condemned to die.

Pioneers in East Texas were as ready to laugh as to weep. They
needed laughter to survive. Life was hard, death ever present.
Large families crowded in houses no bigger than one log room and
a shed room, and scrabbled for a living on land too poor, as they
said, to sprout peas. Constance Rourke says that the "unformed
American nation pictured itself as homely and comic," a statement
that at least partially applies to the Big Thicket.

What did they laugh about? Miss Rourke also says that humor is
a matter of fantasy. Again, this is a statement partially true in the
Big Thicket.

81. East Texas folk musicians.

Much of their humor was inherited along with the traditional ballads. Far back into history English children had laughed at the fantasy of "Frog Went A-Courting." It was also a laughing song for children in the Big Thicket, especially in lines like:

> Next came in was a bumblebee,
> Playing his fiddle on his knee.

Another kind of fantasy appears in the ballad "Rosemary One Time" (Rosemary and Thyme), which is a version of "Scarborough Fair." The story of it is worth summarizing with some stanzas:

> As you go through that yonder's town,
> Rosemary one time,
> Admire your address to that fair lady
> And ask her to be a true lover of mine.
> Tell her to make me a cambric shirt,
> Rosemary one time,
> Without a seam or a seamster's work
> And then she will be a true lover of mine.

He sets several more impossible tasks for her. She responds with her own test.

> Tell him to plant me one acre of corn,
> Rosemary one time,
> Between the salt water and the sea shore
> And then he'll be a true lover of mine.

After he has done a dozen of these tasks, he can come and get his cambric shirt.

In "The Farmer's Curst Wife" the devil comes to the farmer in the field one day and the farmer gives him his scolding wife, with the warning "you can't keep her to save your life." He takes her down to hell and a scene opens up:

> Six little devils a-dragging their chains,
> Saying, "Take her back, pappy, before she
> beats out our brains."

Then there is the final defeat of the devil:

> He packed her all up in a sack
> And like a damned fool went carrying her back.

And the victory of the farmer:

> The old man went whistling across the hill,
> Saying, "If the devil won't have her I'll be
> damned if I will."

Another song for a laugh is the story of the old man who sent his wife to work in the field because he thought he could do more of her work in one day than she could do in three. She tells him he has to "feed the old speckled hen," "milk the old brindle cow," "churn the milk in the churn," and so forth. He does all the jobs wrong and gladly yields housework to his wife.

Some of the humor was based on sheer nonsense. "Fair Noddingham Town," a song inherited from England, is typical.

> I started one day to Fair Noddingham town,
> A-riding a horse like walking before,
> With a little nigger drummer a-beating a drum
> With his heels in his pocket before he could run.

And another stanza is reminiscent of Stephen Foster's "Oh, Susanna."

> It rained and it hailed and it snowed and it blowed;
> Ten thousand around me, I sat there alone;
> I called for a bottle to drive sadness away;
> I stifled in dust and it rained all that day.

"A little nigger drummer" is no doubt an American addition to the song.

Much of the frontier humor demonstrates an ability of the people to laugh at themselves. They left one frontier for another in search of a dream—a dream that too often faded into hard reality. "Hoorah for Arkansas" is a song that shows both sides of the coin. The first stanza is full of the dream:

> They say there is a land
> Where crystal waters flow
> That'll cure a man sick or well
> If he will only go.
> We're coming, Arkansas,
> We're coming, Arkansas,
> Our four horse team will soon be seen
> On the road to Arkansas.

A later stanza shows the reality:

They raise their 'baccer patch,
The women all smoke and chaw;
Eat hog and hominy and poke for greens
Way down in Arkansas.
We're leaving Arkansas,
We're leaving Arkansas,
Our four horse team will never be seen
On the roads of Arkansas.

Life on the frontier in Arkansas was tough. It was tougher in Texas, as a song called "Come All You Mississippi Girls" (or Missouri girls) shows.

Come all you Mississippi girls and listen to my noise—
Don't you marry those Texas boys . . .
Let me tell you how they dress:
An old black-dyed shirt and that's the very best,
An old straw hat more brim than crown
And that's how those Texans dress . . .
When they go to cook I'll tell you what they do,
They build up a fire high as your head,
Scratch out the ashes and pile 'em on the bread . . .
Come to the table, thought for to eat,
All they had was a big chunk o' meat,
Cooked half done and tough as a maul,
And old ash cake baked brown and all.
One old knife and nary a fork,
Sawed for an hour and couldn't make a mark;
Kept on sawing till I got it on the floor—
Up with my foot and kicked it out the door.

One of the most remarkable pieces of humor to be found in the Big Thicket is the ballad of Davy Crockett. In the version recorded there he is no longer the hero of the Alamo. He is the wild folk character created in the quarter of a century after his death by the folk mind and made familiar to all America by Davy Crockett almanacs. In this version he is "half horse, half coon, and half sky rocket," and he is teamed up with someone called "Pompey Smash," a Negro minstrel character. They go out hunting, without a gun because Davy can grin a 'coon crazy. Out in the woods "Davy found a squirrel, sitting on a pine log eating sheep sorrel." Davy braces against Pompey Smash's heel and begins grinning. The squirrel does not move but Davy thinks pieces of bark fly around his head. They see that Davy has grinned a knot off a tree instead of a squirrel. Pompey Smash laughs and then they fight till both their heads are missing: "he had bit off my head and I had swallowed his'n."

Characters directly out of Negro minstrelsy are a part of Big Thicket humor. Old Joe Clark and Old Dan Tucker are good examples. "Old Joe Clark" appears as a play-party song:

> Old Joe Clark is dead and gone,
> I hope he's doing well;
> (I hope he's gone to hell)
> He made me wear the ball and chain
> Till it made my ankles swell.

This usually appears as a refrain between stanzas such as:

> I went down to Old Joe's house;
> He was sick in bed;
> Rammed my finger down his throat
> And pulled out a chicken head.

"Old Dan Tucker" also appears as a play-party game. One stanza is enough to show the kind of humor in it:

> Old Dan Tucker, big and fat,
> Washed his face in my old hat;
> Dried his face on a wagon wheel;
> Died with a toothache in his heel.

And then the refrain, which in some play-party games was the "promenade home."

> Get out of the way for Old Dan Tucker,
> He's too late to get his supper;
> Supper's over, dinner's cooking,
> Left old Dan standing a-looking.

82. East Texas folk musicians.

In minstrelsy, Old Dan Tucker is nearly always the shiftless ne'er-do-well. In some play-party games, at the end of the dance Old Dan Tucker is left in the middle with a hand to his eyes, having lost all partners, looking hopeless for one to appear.

Marriage is frequently the butt of the joke, as this song shows:

I am an old miser all tattered and damned,
And oh, and oh, from Ireland I came;
I married a maid both twenty and one,
And the very next morning my sorrows begun.
Oh, what shall I do to get rid of my pain,
I wish to my Lord I was single again;
How I wish my coffin was laid
Before I had married this silly young maid.

In a way, the woman has the last word.

When I was single, marrying was my crave;
Now I am married, Lord, I'm troubled to my grave.
Two little children lying in bed
Both of them so hungry, Lord, they cain't hold
    up their head

Cows are to milk and the spring's to go to,
No one to help me, Lord, I have it all to do,
Gee, I wish I was a single girl again.

When I played this song for Roy Bedichek he said, "I can't laugh at it for crying." In a way he was passing judgment on the humor of these people. The laughing is so often close to crying. In this respect, the Big Thicket is not so different from most of the American frontier. Nevertheless, it is a place unique in my collecting experience.

Some people who came to the Big Thicket said they had come to the back side of creation; others said they had come to the jumping off place. Whatever they said, the Trinity River was in many ways a boundary in the western migration. West of it the land was different—prairie, plain, open country. West of it, people could not hem their settlements in with bayous, and swamps, and thickets. Nor could they preserve their language and lore as untouched as it remained in the Big Thicket.

# FROM MOSS HILL

BY MARGARET L. HEWETT

*When I first started reading Mrs. Hewett's stories I was impressed by her ability to break every known law of English spelling, punctuation, and grammar; when I finished I was impressed by her ability to tell a good story well. She has captured a fine flavor of the Thicket, and I am still not sure whether her success is in spite of or because of her style. Every time I tried editing these tales from Moss Hill (between Liberty and Rye on state highway 146) and translating them into traditional English, I lost some of that flavor. So I quit and turned them over to the general editor and the printer as a challenge to the first's sense of phonetics and the second's ability as a type setter.*

*I don't believe that the unorthodox mechanics will bother the reader very much. The experience should be much like one's first experience with a sixteenth century manuscript or facsimile. He might, however, have trouble with point of view; sometime it's hard to tell who is talking. Usually Mrs. Hewett identifies herself with the main character and speaks in the first person through him. But she never intrudes; the character's personality is always the dominant one. Mrs. Hewett knows these people, and she and her characters have hacked and plowed through many years and miles of the Big Thicket. They fit the scene.—F.E.A.*

83. Mrs. Margaret L. Hewett.

## *Old Man Whaley and the Hog Stampede*

This old Negro man was Ninety years old when he told me this story.

his name was Reubin Banks, he was born at Whaley cove four miles North east of Moss Hill, and lived in this vinecity all his life.

when he was big enough to sit in the Saddle Mr, Whaley would take him hunting wild Hogs and cattle, they hunted all over towards Strain that was about ten miles South East of Batson.

He told me old man Whaley was a big fat man, and rode a very high spirited horse in fact a Stallion, he was always trying to pitch, we had the dogs after a bunch of hogs three or four years old i would judge, for they had long tushes, we was running through the brush as fast as we could, but the Hogs would circle back ever so often, the dogs was giving them plenty of room while trying to worry them down. Mr, Whaley told me to keep after them, for he was getting tired chasing right back over the same trail. he told me he would take a stand and when they come out by him he would shoot them down with his Winchester, or at least as many as he could before they got by.

Sure enough they turned right back towards Mr, Whaley, i was pulling leather and dodging trees and brush trying to stay in sight of the Hogs, i heard one shot then i heard no more, but i kept right on going, i passed right clost to where i had left Mr, Whaley then i heard him hollering for me, i wheeled around and rode back, i could hear him cussing with all the language the Lord had forbidden me to use, when i got to him, he hollowed Rube get me down, this dammed Stallion pitched me off and run, when i started shooting, them Hogs was coming at me so fast and i was so scared i like to not climbed this tree. I folded over and tried to keep from laughing but it come out any way then i couldent stop, Mr, Whaley yelled you dam black heathern, get me out of this tree, and stop that Panther howl. I got off my Horse but i couldent stop laughing, for Mr, Whaley was sitting right flat on the ground, with his arms and legs locked around the tree, and all them wild hogs had passed him by while he was thinking he was climbing the tree, he threatend to hang me to a rafter in the barn if i ever told what he done. any time i heard him cussing that stallion i knew he was thinking about the hogs.

This all happened in 1883 Whaley had over one hundred Slaves or so the story goes but Whaley cove is still here and the lake they claim was dug with slaves.

Reuben Banks told me this story in 1950.

The Whaleys is buried out at Whaley cove, they have Grandchildren living here clost to me.

### Lizzie Albrow and Indian Gold

I was eight years old and remember well when the Indians ust to come through here on their way to the coast, they always had a bag of Gold Dust to trade for the things they wanted, my father was still working for the son of the man, that owned him during Slave times, all the Negro people taken the name of their

Master, my Father told us kids, his master was good to him, and his Pappy before him.

I was born on this very place, my Mother and Father was to, we farmed Cotton for our boss man, i was to young to go to the Field, so i stayed home and minded the little ones. if something went wrong i would go out and beat a huge plow sweep with a rod of iron, soon Mother would come to the House.

my job was to wash the dishes and sweep the floor, with an old sage broom, and this work must be done or i would get the broom used on me.

one day i was sweeping when i heard the Dog start barking, i went to the door to see what was wrong, i got the scare of my life, for a big Indian was outside the gate, i slammed the door shut, and thought of getting to the sweep to ring for my Mother but the Indian was between me and it.

He started calling to me in english, telling me he would not hurt me, and that he had something for my Pa. I eased the door open a mite and peeked out at him he was holding up a little bag, I didnot venture out, he told me he wanted to trade us the little bag for Coffee. I still didnot go out, he stooped down and picked up one little basket from the ground, i'll trade you this for a little Coffee he told me, it was the prettiest thing i had ever seen, so i eased out on the porch, he held the Basket up so i could see it, i lost all my fear and went on out to the gate, i held out my hand for the basket but he said, no you give Coffee first, i dashed back into the kitchen and got him a cup of Green parched coffee, he gave me the basket and went away.

I was afraid to tell Ma and Pa what i had done, so i hid the basket, the next day another Indian come, this time he had a load of baskets, i traided him a cup of coffee for each basket until i ran out of coffee, when he left i had eight baskets, and the one from the day before made nine.

when my mother and father come in from the field and went to make coffee, they raised the roof, i had to tell them what went with the coffee, the Indians was camped about one half mile away so pa went to his boss man and had him to go and get our coffee back, i

84. Wagon Wheel.

bawled all night because i lost my baskets, and partly from the pain in my bottom, where pa had used the razor strap.

Another Man by the name of Arthur Strahan, lived way out in East woods, he told me [Mrs. Hewett] his Grandmother was full blood Indian, and married his grandfather, which was a Frenchman, his Grandmother told him of the Indians coming down from Woodville in the fall of the year, and bringing enough Gold dust with them to buy their supplies, through the winter. they camped down on the coast but he didnot know where. he is dead now but has sons and Daughters living around here.

He told me, his Grandmother told him about the Indians coming down one fall and over clost to Arizona Creek which runs between Votaw and Moss Hill, the Indians was jumped by a bunch of outlaws, and shot up pretty bad, the Indian that was carrying the Gold got away and hid it in a big Hollow Hickory Tree, clost to where they named the place Indian Springs, he was wounded bad but before he died he told where it was hid, as best he could, they never did find it, or so the story went. Arthur Strahan died last year but he hunted the Hickory Tree as long as he lived. So that makes two people that has told me about the Indians bringing Gold down from woodville.

### Fount Simmons and Old Ellis
### and the Mad Dog

Bemie Bailey an old man of 81, told me this.

When i was a youngen, we lived, at Big Sandy clost to Dollardsville, there was a man lived clost to us, the first time i seen him he rode up to the house, and i was playing clost to the gate, the man rolled down off his Horse and started crawling towards me, it like to have scared the daylights out of me.

I ran for the house yelling for Pa and Ma, they come out on the porch, and asked the Man what was rong, nothing he told them, i am your new neighbor, and i am paralized from the waist down, so i have to crawl instead of walking, the man's name was Fant Simmons, he lived by us for thirty years, him and Pa coon hunted to-

85. Uncle Fount Simmons (Courtesy Mrs. J. A. McKim).

gether killed Deer and Bear, Mr, Fant would take a stand sitting on his horse, when a Deer come by he would shoot him, then he would rope the Deer and drag it to a tree with a limb hanging out he would throw the rope over the limb and drag the Deer up high enough, he could ride under it and load it onto his Saddle, he told us one time, he had killed over seven hundred Deer in his lifetime, and had loaded them all that way, he had never walked so it never bothered him.

He would have one of his Sons train a horse for him in the way he was to be used he wouldent have any color but, bay, he said they was of a gentle nature and was not likely to shy away from any thing, once trained.

I liked to hear him talk, so when him and Pa got to talking i would back up against a porch post and keep quiet, so as not to miss one word.

86. A pole barn.

when i was a boy, he told us, my pa had an old negro slave, he
could outrun any race horse, that was the runningest Negro i ever
seen, he would pull off his hat and take off down the trail and me
hot on him with the horse, if i didnt quirt that horse, old Ellis
would out run him.

One spring, i remember, there was a big Mad Dog scare up, every body watched out for them, Pa wouldent let us kids walk any

where, we either rode the horse or stayed home, every man carried his Gun to church.

one of the kids was sick, on this sunday night, so we all stayed home, old Ellis told Pa he was going to Church, take the mare, Pa told him, it is dangerous to walk, no suh, Ellis said, aint no mad dog gwing to catch me.

About ten oclock we heard the worst racket on the porch, Pa called out, but no answer, by that time i had crawled across the floor to the door, Pa opened it and there layed old Ellis, he couldent talk he was babbling, but we couldent understand him, Pa got him up and taken him to the kitchen, Ma fixed some Coffee and held it for him to drink, we finally got out of him, he had heard the swish of a dog right behind him, when he started to run it chased him all the way up to our yard gate. Pa grabbed his old gun and headlight, you couldent see twenty feet with it for it had two little wicks, set into the base and an old rusty reflector. Ma cautioned Pa about going outside with the thing, but he went any way.

he looked around a little and come back saying he would get up a hunt when it got daylight. Old Ellis slept on the kitchen floor that night he was so scared.

the next morning Pa rode to some of the Neighbors, and told them what had happened, they got their Guns and followed Pa back to our house, Pa told Ellis to get a horse and come along, no sir he told him i is going to walk, i can run or climb a tree if that dog gets after me again, come on then Pa told him, but you walk ahead of the horses then we can see you, about an hour later Pa come back and was laughing fit to bust, he said old Ellis was walking ahead, all at once he started yelling i hear him coming again, Ellis had started to run, Pa and the others run him down and roped him, then discovered, what he had heard swishing was the legs of his new britches rubbing together, as he walked, ma declared she would make him wash the next britches she made him, to keep all such nonsence down. all the men round about hurrawed old Ellis so much he never went to Church again, a few years later he died and Pa and some of the neighbors, buried him out in the grove clost to the Peach orchid, Ma tended his Grave as long as she lived.

## Bailey's Bears

The Baileys was born and raised at Big Sandy in Polk County, Bemie Bailey told me this. he is 84 years old.

he said during the Cival War, his Dady was a Cournal, while he was gone off to war his wife was staying, by herself with three small children, they raised the corn and fattened their Hogs, their selves, many nights she had to take a pine torch and go to the Hog pen and run the bears off, they got so bad she had to turn the Hogs out, so they could bunch together in order to fight the Bears off.

She killed a Hog and cooked the fat out, they did not have any floor in the House: it was all dirt, one night she heard something scratching, she got up and found a Bear was digging under the wall right where she had her grease barrel sitting she was afraid to move it back, for fear the bear would get into the cabin and kill one of her children, so she already had a little fire in the fire place, she got her old iron tea kettle, and filling it with grease she had it boiling, by the time the Bear had dug enough to stick his head through, she pourd the hot grease on his nose and eyes, he let out a roar and jerked his head back, but he like to have torn the cabin down, he went so crazy, he screamed and beat the walls for an hour they didnot get any more sleep that night.

when her husband come home he raised and trained a bunch of Hound Dogs to run Bear, his oldest boy was twelve years old by this time, the bear would still come to the hog pens but the dogs would run them off. one morning just about sun up, they heard a hog squeling, out in the woods, they knew a bear had caught him, so Mr, Bailey called his dogs and taking the oldest boy with him he headed for the woods. Son, he told him, i will put you on a stand for i know the Bear will come through here, you can shoot him when he comes. Bailey went on into the woods and soon the Dogs struck the Bear's trail, sure enough he made for the direction the boy was in, he passed on and Bailey never heard any shots, when he got to where he had left the boy, son he said, i didnot hear any shot, no said the boy, he didnot come by here. Sir you will not lie to me, Bailey told him, for i will whip you quicker then for any

87. A Thicket marsh.

other thing you do. the boy hung his head and said, well sir i was
up that tree but my gun was laying on the ground.

### Honey Jones' Grandchildren

My son and his folks lived here with me, for quite
a spell, but the youngens was lots of help. I remember one time we

had to have some fresh meat and lard, i told the kids to go drive up some of my shoats and i would kill one, they come back with about half dozen of the wildest shoats in the woods, we could not get them into the pen, i had one shell for my six shooter, i taken dead aim at that shoat and hit him, he started squeling and run off through the briar patch, take to him and dont let him get away, i told them, one of the gals the twelve year old started out with two of the boys right behind her, right through that briar patch they all went, sounded like a heard of cattle, i could hear them hollering for a mile away, they was gone for around a hour then i heard them coming back, the biggest boy had the shoat across his shoulder, i could see the blood running down the front of the boy, but felt satisfied because i could still shoot my old gun good enough to kill a hog, the boy throwed the shoat down in front of me and its head was nearly cut off, what happened to him i asked, well i had only hit that shoat in the nose and give it a good start, them youngens had run it down and forced it into old boggy lake, they waded out and caught him and the oldest boy had cut its throat with his daddys straight razor, my boy never could shave with that razor no more, and that boy got the tail beat off him.

# THE SARATOGA LIGHT

BY FRANCIS E. ABERNETHY

The Old Bragg Road with its mysterious Light turns left off Farm Road 1293 about seven miles west of Honey Island and heads straight for Saratoga, in the heart of the Big Thicket. The road itself is sandy, graded, and pretty well ditched, and is wide enough for two cars to pass. It is seven miles long and as straight as a rifle barrel. Loblolly pines that will make poles and saw logs in a few years grow right up close to the road on both sides, and occasional bogs hold their water and snakes and frogs tight up against the road bed. Sweet-gum sprouts, yaupon, and palmetto, growing thick in patches and always rustling, fringe the road, that after a light night rain carries the sandy signs of all the 'coon and cats and 'possums and armadillos that take their nightly stroll along its trail. A set of broad, splay-footed tracks show where a big old buck deer has eased up to the edge of the palmetto and pine, scanned the road to see that all was calm, and then sauntered down the middle, between the tire tracks, just taking his pleasure walking in the sand.

Before 1901 this was all thicket and cypress brake and shallow clay pan, holding water and growing thick with ty-vine and saw briars, and choked in the shallow ponds with baygalls a ribbon snake couldnt wiggle through. Then the Santa Fe railroad shot a line between Bragg and Saratoga and cut a right of way and brought progress through this part of the Thicket in the form of

88. The Old Bragg Road—the ghost road.

the old "Saratoga." It made a trip a day to Beaumont and back with people and cattle and oil and logs, and it lasted till the tracks were no longer needed for hauling the oil from the Saratoga field and the virgin pine from the Thicket.

Sante Fe road crews pulled the rails in 1934 and for many years the old tram road was just another bad road that tunneled through the Thicket, which would have taken it over, but there was still some traveling back and forth between Bragg and Saratoga. And there were the hunters—the fox runners and cat hunters and those that chased the deer. They used the road because it carried them into some of the densest woods in the Big Thicket.

The old tram road was one long bog during the rainy season, and the brush crowded insistently in on it, always trying to elbow the travelers off. And then there was the Light. Cecil Overstreet and some of the old-timers and their offshoots say that the Light has been showing up as far back as they can remember, fifty years or more. Sometime in the uncalendared past, Harry Broom, a Sara-toga barber, and Joe Martin were running the fox one night and had stationed themselves by a pine-knot fire on the edge of the road bed to listen to the hounds. During the race the Light showed up. Harry throught it was a fire hunter or somebody with a flash-light walking down the road, so he hollered at it. When he got no answer, he decided he'd better investigate, so he eased on down the road to where he thought the light was. Just as he got there the Light faded out and disappeared; Harry and Joe Martin left soon after. The two hunters told their story and were plagued by the sceptics, but after that, other hunters and late wanderers on the road saw the Light and verified—and amplified—Harry's report.

One lady came back from Waco to the Thicket in 1961 just to see the Light again. She reported seeing it when the tracks were still on the road bed. She said that when she was five years old and her father worked on the railroad, she, her mother, a neighboring lady, and the rest of the children all walked down the tracks to meet her father when he got off from work one evening. The Light appeared and scared them all into hysterics, so she said, and the belief that the world was coming to an end. "Warty" Lewis tells a

229

story his grandfather, George Lewis, told him about the Light, which he saw back in the 'thirties. The elder Lewis was coming up the Bragg Road from Saratoga late one night in a wagon when the Light suddenly appeared and rushed down between the team. The horses panicked and broke loose, leaving George and the wagon in the ditch. The walk back to Saratoga in the dark was as long as the silence and side-long glances that followed his telling the tale.

For fifty years, more or less, the Thicketites of the Honey Island and Saratoga area have accepted the fact that there is a Light on the old Bragg tram road. The young folks considered the road to be their particular Lover's Lane, especially after it was graded and improved in 1952. They got used to the Light, which they variously described as red, white, blue, green, and combinations; as hot and cold; as floating, darting, leaping, and stationary. The Light was always a good excuse to go there and park. Then in the dog days of August in 1960, when there wasn't much to do, young people from all over Hardin and Jefferson counties began drifting to the road, and talk of the Light grew strong. Archer Fullingim—publisher, editor, and printer of *The Kountze News*—took the story and with the reportorial assistance of Mrs. Geraldine Collins of Saratoga he investigated, analyzed, and publicized the Light until about everybody in East Texas and even beyond the piney woods knew about the Old Bragg Road and the Big Thicket Light.

Light-seers poured onto the road by the hundreds. People of all ages and intellects came to see and test their belief in the supernatural. They shot at it, they chased it, and they tested it with litmus paper and geiger counters. A preacher harangued the road's multitudes from the top of his car, marking the Light as an ill omen of the world's impending doom. Traveling the road became hazardous at night, and the sheriff's department made periodical rounds to keep some semblance of order. There were some nights when the Light didn't show at all, and often it was seen but vaguely; but for the most part it was there to inspire stories that could be passed on, to change and grow at the will and imagination of the story teller. According to reports that came out of the Thicket during this period, the Light went wild. It chased cars; it floated over

89. Arden Hooks in the Thicket.

the hoods and cut out engines; it burned hands and scorched car tops. Several people reported running over it, and others said that it ran over them, one young man stating that it got on top of his car and made "odd noises and tromping sounds."

All sorts of explanations were offered by the philosopher-scientists of the Bragg Road. The hardest minded of the lot insisted that the Light was the reflection of car lights as they made a bend on the Saratoga road where the Bragg Road butted into it. Opponents countered this theory by pointing out that the Light had been seen before the Saratoga road had many cars on it, that Model-T headlights wouldn't shine far enough to be seen the necessary four or five miles down the Bragg Road, and that the brush was so thick along the road bed that a light couldn't shine through it to the area where the Light was usually seen. Physicists and biochemists were invited in by Editor Fullingim, and there was a vague but general agreement among this group that the Light was gaseous. Dr. Edwin S. Hayes, head of the biology department at Lamar State College in Beaumont, said he thought that the Light was a low grade of gas, commonly found in swampy areas. But there was opposition even to science. The Thicketites were well acquainted with swamp fire and will-of-the-wisps, and this was nothing like it; the scientists knew not of what they spoke.

In spite of this flurry of speculation, nothing was proven. Neither teenagers nor scientists were able to lay the ghosts that old stories had peopled Bragg Road with. There was some talk that the Light was a mystical phenomenon that typically frequented areas where treasure was buried, and that some early Spanish conquistadors had cached a golden hoard in the Thicket but had failed to return for it. Some said that the Light was a little bit of fire that never was extinguished after the Kaiser Burnout; others said that it was the ghost of a man shot during the Burnout, when the Confederate soldiers fired part of the Thicket to flush out those Jayhawkers who weren't interested in fighting for the South. There's one story about a railroad man who was decapitated in a train wreck on this part of the Saratoga line; they found his body but never could locate his head, and the body continues to roam up and down the right of way looking for the lost member. And one tale tells that the Light comes from a spectral fire pan carried by a night hunter who got lost in the Big Thicket years ago. He still wanders, never stopping to rest, always futilely searching for a way out of the mud and briars.

Another tale of grislier proportions deals with what is loosely referred to as "the Mexican cemetery," about a quarter of a mile off the north end of the Bragg Road bed. Buried there is part of a crew of Mexicans who were hired to help cut the right of way and lay the tracks. But, rumor has it, the foreman of the road gang, rather than pay them a large amount of accumulated wages, killed the men and kept the money. They were hurriedly interred in the dense woods nearby, from whence come their restless, uneasy souls clouded in ghostly light to haunt that piece of ground that cost them their lives.

And there was the man who watched fascinated as the Sante Fe sent the "Saratoga" and the "Somerville" steaming and whistling through the Big Thicket. He sold his farm and parted with everything that he couldn't pack in a suitcase, and he went to work on the railroad. He was devoted to the line, and he became a brakeman on the "Saratoga." But his romantic life as a railroad man was relatively short lived, and when the Santa Fe began to cut down on its runs, he found himself without a job or prospects. He died soon after, but his lonesome and troubled spirit still walks the road bed with its brakeman's lantern, looking for the life that left him behind.

The romantics and the tale spinners in the Big Thicket probably know a lot more stories about the Light than these. And there'll probably be a lot more tales circulating before it's all over, because as long as there's a Light, there'll be people looking at it and trying to figure it out. A lot of folks will lose a night's worth of T.V. and some sleep just to go there and prove the Light isn't so, and all the time they'll be hoping that it is. Then they'll put it through all the tests, dead set on showing that there is a physico-chemical explanation, and all the time they'll be secretly hoping that they'll fail. In the middle of a Thicket full of miracles they'll run up and down the road hollering, "It's a fake," and all the time they're meaning, "Give me a sign." Because if they can believe in the supernatural of a Big Thicket Ghost, then they can more easily accept the mystery of the Holy Ghost—and life will add another dimension.

# INDEX

Abba Mingo: and the Corn-Grinder, 51–52; prayed to, 73

agriculture: Indians taught techniques of, 49–50; early practices of, in Thicket, 62, 112

Ais, the (Indians): 173

Alabama-Coushatta: 36–37; associated with Thicket, 33; tribes joined, 45

Alabama-Coushatta Reservation: 36–37; lands purchased for, 39–40; present boundaries of, 44–45

Alabamas (Indians): 36–37; in the 18th century, 35; come to Texas, 35–38; in Texas history, 35–42

Alabama Trace: 36–37

Albrow, Lizzie: and Indian gold, 217–220

Allen, George: as Thicket cattleman, 121–122

Allums, Jim: 191

Anadarko Indians: massacre of, 35

Angelina County, Texas: as part of Thicket, 201

Angelina River: Indian village on, 39

Antone, Chief (Alabama): appeals to Houston, 40

Arizona Creek: Indians shot near, 220

Arline, Jonah: ghost of, 190

Arroyo Hondo: as boundary of Thicket, 201

Atakapans (Indians): in Thicket, 11, 33

Audubon, John James: discusses passenger pigeons, 29–30

Austin, Stephen F.: map by, 173–174

Bad Luck Creek: 13; described, 81; origin of name of, 88, 90

—, Battle of: versions of, 75–78; Cordelia Sutton's story of, 79–91

Bailey, Bemie: tells of Ellis and mad dog, 220

"Barbara Allen": 206

Barclay, James: Indians on land of, 39; as agent for Alabamas, 40; Governor Runnels' letter to, 40

Barclay Village (Indian): 36–37

Barefoot Man of Caney Head, the: 22

Barwick, Hamp: on Tarkington stampede, 120–122

Batson, Texas: oil boom in, 137, 144–154; boom-town law in, 145

Batson Prairie: as Thicket boundary, 14; the Guedrys of, 67; Buck Hooks' farm on, 107; on Louisiana trail, 138–139

Battise Trace: 36–37

Battise Village (Indian): 36–37

Bayou Boeuf: Alabamas on, 54

Bazile, Mr. (Dr. Mud): described, 139; work of, at Springs Hotel, 176–180

bear: seen in Thicket, 9; in Thicket folklore, 26; in Indian myth, 50–51, 53; hunts for, 97–100, 126–136, 224–225; Carter Hart kills, 123–124; decline of, 136

bear oil: sold at Drew's Landing, 72–73

Beaumont, Texas: 70; as seaport, 114; visitors to Sour Lake from, 180; near boundary of Thicket, 210; as railroad terminal, 229

Beaumont clay: as Thicket soil, 17–18

*Beaumont Enterprise, The:* Grandma Harrison story in, 70; Dean Tevis as writer for, 75; Kaiser's Burnout in, 75; brings news to Honey Island, 158; Ruth Scurlock as writer for, 169

Beaver Creek: 13

Bedichek, Roy: 214

*Belle of Texas, The:* at Drew's Landing, 71

Belreaux Slough: Hooks settle on, 182

Belt, Sam: as Indian agent, 173

Bevil, Dr. John: 145

Bevil, Leake: on cattle hunt, 192

Big Buck Saloon: 141